25th Aug 2009

TOWER
you rogue ⟶

100 REASONS TO VOTE YES TO LISBON II

I'm doing all this
sober from your
example.
Great to see you
at Oran.
Nick

Published by Trashface Books, Dublin, Ireland

ISBN: 978-1-906527-18-1

www.trashface.com

ABOUT THE AUTHOR

Nick McGinley is a Dublin-based writer. His comedy sketch show *Hoarse Throat Soothers* co-written with Shane O'Neill won 'Spirit of the Unfringed Festival' in 2008. He has been a radio essayist for *Spectrum* and *Frequencies* on RTE Radio 1 and has written stage & radio plays, TV scripts and screenplays. He is currently working on a collection of short stories.

Contents

19 National sovereignty is strengthened.

20 The scope of legal redress for European citizens is widened.

21 Lisbon will not turn the EU into a superstate.

22 Better balance of power between the Commission and the Parliament

23 Improves mutual emergency assistance for member states

24 Lisbon consolidates the Union.

25 For the money

26 Lisbon protects asylum seekers.

27 The EU shall have legal personality.

28 Gives smaller member states better levels of representation

29 Ensures protection for workers, public services and competition

30 Allows the EU to expand...cautiously

31 Lisbon won't lead to increased militarism.

32 The Treaty can always be changed, but only by 'us'.

33 It will piss off the British Conservative Party.

34 It'll piss off Sinn Féin.

35 If we're not in the heart of Europe, we can't influence European policy.

Contents

55 Finally, that annoying and confusing difference between the E.C. and E.U. is resolved.

56 Greater economic opportunities

57 More efficient information-sharing between member states

58 St. Columbanus would want you to vote for Lisbon.

59 If Lisbon isn't ratified, we will revert to the Treaty of Nice.

60 Carla Bruni wants us to. And what Carla wants, Carla gets.

61 Other states' sympathy with Ireland's concerns is finite.

62 The European Investment Bank has a €300 million loan fund for small business.

63 Protects human rights #2

64 National vetoes are protected.

65 If you vote yes to Lisbon it'll piss off Declan Ganley.

66 Lisbon protects schools & hospitals from takeover by greedy capitalists.

67 Euronews is mesmerising entertainment, even if you're only slightly stoned.

68 Lisbon has nothing to do with tax.

69 It'll improve our reputation in Europe.

70 Even the naysayers say Yes to Lisbon II.

Contents

87 Lisbon reinforces the legitimacy of the UN.

88 Better organised crime prevention

89 It'll help EU Members combat domestic violence.

90 Cheaper air travel

91 Because Ulick says nyet!

93 Biffo came back from Brussels with the protocol bacon.

94 Helps the EU to be the bulwark against bad big business practice

95 The Lisbon Treaty hasn't changed; everything else has.

96 The EU's got funky agencies like the Rapid Alert System for Consumer Goods.

97 Joe Higgins will have to engage constructively with EU institutions.

98 It will consign Czech President Vaclav Klaus to the same skip in which the pan-European Libertas party now resides.

99 MEPs' expenses have been comprehensively reformed. Or have they?

100 So that Lisbon can get back to being a lovely place and not a byword for tedium

ACKNOWLEDGEMENTS

Thanks to Shane Griffin our European Affairs Analyst, Siobhan Gaffney for her Legal Advice, Antony Farrell of The Lilliput Press, Martyn Turner for the heaving beauty on the cover and Olly O'Neill (olly@ollyoneill.com) for his sterling design and typesetting work.

Thanks also to Ruth Deasy at EU House, Simon Carswell, John Downes, Conor Kavanagh, Gavin O'Donoghue, Jamie Smyth and Zoe Comyns.

AUTHOR'S NOTE ON TEXT

The Treaty citations at the bottom of each reason are laid out as follows: Treaty of Lisbon: Old Article No. [New No.] Treaty on European Union or Treaty on the Functioning of the European Union)

If a quotation is not cited as a footnote, it has come from a direct interview with the author.

1 We'll have focused, dedicated and consistent EU leadership for the first time.

Lisbon provides for a President of the European Council who isn't also a national leader who has to deal with all of the demands of his/her own State. This will mean a leader who can properly serve the areas where the States have conferred competence on the EU and who won't be always looking to how it affects the home country. It's the difference between having a good friend whom you can rely on and one with a really possessive partner.

This will also mean we'll get away from the pass-the-parcel game every six months with a Council President who can be elected for up to five years[1], providing a stable, coherent Council leadership that isn't chopping and changing. Six months? What's that about? What Brussels barmat was that written on? You've barely feng-shuied your office and tried out the local phone-a-pizza line by the time you're turfed out at present.

"Since he came to power in 2000, the President of Russia, President Putin has been faced with no less than sixteen different Presidents of the Council and two Commission Presidents only."[2]

Commission President Barroso called this 'rapidly changing gallery' of Council Presidents a barrier to coherence of policy and vision. The Council Presidency under Lisbon will mean that the domestic strife of host countries like the collapse of

---

1   2 ½ years with the option of running for a second term.
2   José Manuel Barroso 93rd Plenary session, National Forum on Europe, 17 April 2008

the Czech government this year will no longer have a dispro-
portionate impact on Europe as a whole.

The Council Members - each State leader - vote for the President by unanimity. If the European Council President was
elected in a Europe-wide poll instead, it would disadvantage
smaller States like Ireland on a popula-tion basis, so we don't want to go down that road.

6 months? What's that about? What Brussels barmat was that written on?

Many Irish people experienced a quiet thrum of pride puffing out the chest when Pat Cox was elected President of the
European Parliament and when Ireland's 2004 stewardship
of the Council Presidency went smoothly. Now how about an
Irish politico going for the gold? Many Irish politicians have
scaled the heights of the EU institutions in our thirty-six years
of membership, but the chances of our fellow Member States
voting for an Irish Council President if we reject the Treaty
again, whose final wording was agreed on our watch in 2004,
would be slim indeed. With the Council President convening
the meeting of all the State leaders only twice every six months,
the longer s/he is in the job the better.

TL: Article 9B [15] TEU

2 The EU will have a coherent EU foreign policy deployed through one office.

The High Representative for Foreign Affairs and Security policy will take on two existing jobs: the top position on the Foreign Affairs Council and as Commissioner for External Relations.

This is the Union's 'chief diplomat' who will ensure a greater level of continuity in representing the EU's foreign policy. The High Representative shall be assisted by a European External Action Service, which probably sounds a lot cooler than it's going to be. This service of busy little minions shall work in co-operation with the diplomatic services of the

> This post is equivalent to a super mash-up between Javier Solana's job and the role occupied by Benita Ferraro-Waldner in the Commission.

Member States and comprise officials from relevant departments of the General Secretariat of the Council and of the Commission as well as staff seconded from national diplomatic services of the Member States. In between barking orders at his new multinational servants like 'Green Tea, now!', oder 'Grüne Tee, jetzt! And make sure it's fairtrade!', the High Rep would also articulate the EU's position to the United Nations Security Council.

This post is equivalent to a super mash-up between Javier Solana's job and the role occupied by Benita Ferraro-Waldner in the Commission. The High Rep briefs the European Parliament and in turn take its views into account. He doesn't replace the Foreign Ministers of the Member States, but makes the proposals to the Foreign Affairs Council made up of the Foreign Ministers and acts on their agreed mandate, under a voting regime that rests on the principle of unanimity. So yes, all the States retain the option to veto any of his or her cockamamy proposals.

The High Rep is today only accountable to the Council, but with the double-jobbing as a Commissioner also comes a new accountability to that institution as well. Previously the Commissioner for External Relations would have to be sent with the High Rep whenever he was off in some far-flung locale representing the EU. Now it's going to be one and the same person.

TL: 9B [15], 9D [17], 9E [18] TEU

3 More democratic decision-making for the EU

More decisions are to be made by Qualified Majority Voting (QMV) instead of by unanimity. This will speed up decision-making and transform the lumbering behemoth into a lithe, graceful athlete.

It's a strength of the Treaty that means majority voting will become the general rule reserving unanimity for sensitive issues like defence and taxation. This will ensure the efficient delivery of plans to combat terrorism, cross-border crime, illegal immigration and human trafficking. It will speed up decision-making in the institutions and the EU won't be paralysed at the sweetshop door by

> The EU won't be paralysed at the sweetshop door by the spectre of choosing between a twix and penny bonbons...

the spectre of choosing between a Twix and penny bonbons and about whether the Twix actually qualifies as a bar or a biscuit or if indeed it should be called a Twix in the EU and not perhaps a 'snafu' instead and as for the penny part, that's well out of order in the monetary Eurozone, but where's the romance in 20-cent apple drops?

As the union grew to accommodate twenty-seven (potentially sweet-toothed) members, this movement to consensus decision-making was inevitable to have any sort of efficiency for passing legislation. In unanimity voting, each Member State did not just have one vote, but there was a system of weighted voting in recognition of population size. The EU assigned a specific amount of weighted votes to each Member State with a threshold set for a qualified majority. Each time a new Member State joined, a table of voting weights had to be re-negotiated.

German chancellor Angela Merkel said in Dublin last year "It is true we are making more use of majority voting, because we want a Europe that is able to act."[3]

The Treaty would change the system from 2014 to a qualified or 'double majority', which would be defined as 55 per cent of the members of the EU comprising at least fifteen member States representing 65 per cent of the population of the EU. A proposal can also be blocked if it is opposed by at least four Member States, called a blocking minority. If they applied double majority voting now, the population needed to carry a proposal would be 322 million out of 495, with fifteen out of the twenty-seven States supporting it. The current weighted voting system (255 votes are needed out of a total of 345) will be phased out, but a Member State can request its use until 2014. Needing four States to form a blocking minority further democratises the voting system, as it is impossible for three of the larger States to stop a proposal by dint of population-size alone.

When decisions are made using majority voting, the Member states are sharing sovereignty and when they use unanimity, they are intergovernmental. The EU is moving from an intergovernmental organisation to a union of nations who agree to share some of their sovereignty in areas where it makes sense to pool resources and speak with one voice. The elephants must not step on the mice and the mice must not nibble on the elephants' feet. The smaller nations can set up blocking majorities if they don't agree with a proposal, but no longer can one recalcitrant State repeatedly and continually frustrate progress completely.

---

3   Angela Merkel, NFE, 92nd Plenary session, 14 April 2008, pg. 209

Our former Commissioner David Byrne said that Qualified Majority Voting "reflects, in my view, the dual nature of the Union, being a union of States and of peoples."[4]

The double majority system is more democratic and more effective in comparison with the system employed in the Nice Treaty, since it facilitates the creation of majorities.

TL: Article 9C [16] TEU; Article 205 [238] TFEU

---

4   David Byrne, 91st session, 10 April 2008

4 We will retain our Commissioner.

Ireland will keep its Commissioner in a one-per-Member State Commission Structure under a new guarantee to assuage Ireland's fears of losing out on influence.

The periodic loss of a Commissioner for five years out of every fifteen really would not have lessened each country's influence on EU affairs as the commissioners are not supposed to represent national interests anyway. This is crucial and we either accept that this is how the Commission is run, or persist with a suspicion that it's all only been about national interests; that all along, this island has had no real aim to be part of a larger fellowship of

> ...as our concerns were taken seriously, this is a major concession to Irish fears of loss of influence.

States pooling sovereignty to attain common interests, but that we've been sniggering behind our hands amazed at the largesse in Structural Funds thrown in our direction by this well-meaning, but easily manipulated EU Sugar Daddy.

This Commission structural change would have streamlined the workings of an institution that rocketed from six Commissioners to fifteen to twenty-seven by reducing the number corresponding to two-thirds of the Member States in 2014. So out of the current twenty-seven Commissioners, a rotating eighteen would have remained with the idea that the business of the Commission would run more smoothly. Certainly gone are the days when up until the Nice Treaty, the five largest had the right to two Commissioners.

Before the guarantee was granted, TD Michael McGrath made the point that "It is a huge sacrifice for the larger countries, who previously had two Commissioners to now arrive at a situation where they have one Commissioner for ten out of every fifteen years on an equal basis with Ireland and other small countries."[5]

The same rules apply across the board, so if the largest States aren't worried about taking it in turns to have a member of their own nationality at the Commission table, then we shouldn't have been getting our knickers in a twist about this. But as we did and as our concerns were taken seriously, this is a major concession to Irish fears of loss of influence.

German chancellor Angela Merkel said "We want the Commission to be a body structured according to its responsibilities and not depend on the number of Member States."[6]

We now continue with the situation of twenty-seven Commissioners with not enough portfolios to go around, where each one would table proposals whether they were needed or not to justify their own existence. The appointment of Commissioners changes from being nominated by Member States to them making 'suggestions' to the European Parliament and Council as to whom they would like to see nominated.

"Let me tell you, by the way, traditionally the Commission has been seen as the institution that is more open to the interests of the small and medium-sized Member States because it is really independent. I come from a country, I have many members in my staff also from different countries, but they are not there representing a country. We don't receive instructions from any country. And this is precisely the originality of the

5   National Forum on Europe, 10 April 2008
6   Angela Merkel, National Forum on Europe, 92nd Plenary session, 14 April 2008

European institutions to have such an institution like that."[7]
By the way, Barroso's the ex-Prime Minister of Portugal and until it conquers Brazil again, it isn't one of the power brokers of the Union. Now that the idea of reducing Commissioner numbers has been reversed and it's back to one Commissioner per State, so be it, but it's either set up as an independent body with a nod and a wink, or it has real institutional independence. Otherwise it's still slow and ungainly.

TL: Article 9D [17] TEU; Article 211A [244] TFEU

---

7   José Manuel Barroso, National Forum on Europe, 93rd Plenary session, 17 April 2008

5 Improved scrutiny of the EU

The enhanced role of National Parliaments ensures greater scrutiny of the EU and power to change every proposal.

Commentator Christian Lesquane posits that 'if there are losers and winners in institutional terms, the most significant factor is the increase in the power of national institutions vis-à-vis the EU institutions – a trend exemplified by the new role given to national parliaments.'[8]

For the first time, the parliaments will get any draft legislation and green & white papers from the Commission at the same time as the Council and the European Parliament. The National Parliaments will have eight weeks to provide a reasoned argument to object to EU legislation on the basis of subsidiarity. This means that the National Parliaments get the right to raise objections to draft EU legislation where national or local action would be more effective. The use of EU powers is governed by the principles of proportionality and subsidiarity. Basically this is a 'checks and balances' device to make sure the EU is not overstepping its remit. The Parliaments can vote to issue a 'reasoned opinion' on whether or not a Commission proposal respects this principle of subsidiarity. Each Parliament has two votes in this system. If at least one-third of such votes are issued, the Commission's draft must be reviewed. In the case of proposals in the areas of judicial co-operation in criminal matters and police co-operation, the threshold is just a quarter of the votes. The Commission then can amend or withdraw its proposal, but if it wants to press on with it and either the Council or the European Parliament agrees with the yellow card from the National Parliaments, then the proposal gets stymied.

8   Gillespie in Brown, T. (ed.), *What the Reform Treaty Means*, pg. 106

"It is all very well for a European treaty to confer enhanced powers on national parliaments, but it will only make a real difference if we, in our own National Parliament, do things differently. It is for us members of the National Parliament to reform our ways of working in order to accommodate and make the best use of the additional competences being given to us."[9] Labour leader Eamon Gilmore is right on this – it's up to us.

In 2007, the Oireachtas established a new Joint Committee on European Scrutiny which now works alongside the Joint Committee on European Affairs. The two Joint Oireachtas Committees will have to be allocated the time and resources to be the watchdogs to scrutinise all Commission proposals, so we can't complain that we didn't find the note EU Sugar Daddy slipped under the door seven weeks and six days ago, because it got all bunched up near the hinge and even though we pulled an all-nighter and bounced around the Dáil bar hopped up on goofballs and Jolt cola, we still couldn't get our heads around it in time – that excuse just won't cut it.

The tendency of national politicians to blame 'faceless Brussels bureaucrats' for imperiously issuing EU directives will be no longer be an excuse available to them, if the Oireachtas is properly empowered to monitor EU legislation. The oldest game in town has been to take the credit for popular initiatives that originated in Europe and then play the EU bureaucracy card when unpopular proposals come into force.

TL: Article 8C [12] TEU; Article 61B [69] TFEU; Protocol on the Role of National Parliaments in the European Union; Protocol on the application of the principles of Subsidiarity and Proportionality.

---

9   Eamon Gilmore, Plenary, National Forum on Europe, pg. 34

6 More clout to our directly elected representatives

The enhanced role of the directly elected European Parliament comes about with co-decision being extended into new policy areas.

Co-decision is the procedure by which the Council and the European Parliament enact legislation between them, after the proposals have been brought before them by the Commission (see Reason #22).The words 'consulting the European Parliament' shall be replaced by 'obtaining the consent of the European Parliament'.

100 Reasons asked MEP Proinsias de Rossa what he thought of this development. He stated "I welcome the increased role of the European Parliament in lawmaking, as this enhances the democratic role of those directly elected in what is a fundamental role of a parliament. It will of course involve an intensification of activity by various committees and that will require a re-organisation of the way the Parliament does its business."

This will further increase the importance of European elections in influencing policy-making. In all, the European Parliament gets co-decision in an extra nineteen existing policy areas, like common financial provisions, measures necessary for the use of the Euro, structural funds and agriculture and fisheries policies, legal immigration (including conditions of entry and residence), visas, asylum (some aspects, including conditions for the reception of applicants), judicial co-operation in criminal matters, police co-operation, Eurojust and decisions on Europol and minimum rules on criminal sanctions for serious crime with cross-border aspects.

The European Parliament gains the power of electing the President of the Commission jointly with the Council. It would also vote on the suggestions that the Member governments make for Commissioners, where previously, the National Governments would just nominate them. Lisbon also extends the Parliament's power in deciding the allocation of the EU budget.

Susan George, a French-based No Campaign activist describes the European Parliament as weak as it doesn't have the power to initiate legislation or levy taxes.[10] And yet the Dáil and every other EU national parliament don't have those powers either.

> The European Parliament gets co-decision in an extra 19 existing policy areas.

Governments, not parliaments, levy taxes and propose legislation. Ex-Fine Gael leader Alan Dukes spotted this and pounced, describing it "a tendentious, incomplete and misleading presentation."

The European Parliament powers are greatly enhanced at the expense of the Commission, so that there is more balance between the institutions, giving more clout to the directly elected house of representatives.

TL: Article 9A [14] TEU

---

10   National Forum on Europe, 91st Plenary session, April 10, 2008

7 Neutrality #1

Article 42 protects Irish neutrality.

The Yes Campaign was won in the second Nice treaty by Ireland reaffirming its position outside any mutual defence commitment. Any decision that Ireland was to become part of a Common Defence policy would have to be ratified constitutionally and would require a Yes vote in a separate referendum.

"All the referenda debates that have taken place in this country over the last thirty-five years have one common theme and that is the imminent loss of our neutrality. We have not lost it in the thirty-five years to date and I don't believe that we are going to lose it in the next thirty-five years, and that comes from someone who represents a party that believes we should participate in the common foreign and security policy of Europe and be a full player, and that also disagrees with the concept of a triple lock."[11]

The specific policy stance of the EU neutrals – Ireland, Sweden, Finland, Austria, Cyprus and Malta – is covered by wording introduced into the Maastricht Treaty at Ireland's insistence and repeated in each Treaty revision since then. The Treaty redefines the Petersberg tasks agreed upon at the Amsterdam Treaty (1997), extending them to encompass joint disarmament operations, military advice and post-conflict stabilisation, along with the original priorities of humanitarian aid, rescue, peacekeeping and crisis management. There's a lot of ambivalence with regard to the debate on neutrality: do the Irish people not want our troops to be part of EU forces that could prevent another genocide like Bosnia? Are we not proud of seeing Irish

---

11   Billy Timmins, Fine Gael TD, Chairman's Report. NFE, pg. 16.

soldiers led by Irish Lieutenant General Pat Nash involved in protecting 400,000 fleeing refugees in Chad and other missions watching over dangerously isolated civilians in Kosovo and in the Democratic Republic of Congo?

> Our status as the Switzerland of the Atlantic, the Sweden without the good-looking people, the Austria without the decent beer is intact and unviolated.

Having Irish troops serve in joint EU and UN peacekeeping missions does not slide us into becoming part of a Common Defence policy, unless we vote for it.

"Unanimity remains the rule for security and defence. No crisis management mission can be launched without our assent. Common defence cannot be agreed without our support and is subject to referendum in Ireland," says Pat Cox, the former President of the European Parliament.

The mutual assistance clause states it *'shall not prejudice the specific character of the security and defence policy of certain Member States.'* This wording was first introduced by the Maastricht treaty upon an Irish proposal and its effect is to allow Ireland to make its own decisions, taking account of its policy of military neutrality. The Irish declaration on traditional military neutrality was agreed during the European Council in Seville – it stands.

General Secretary of the Civil Public & Services Union, Blair Horan, puts it succinctly: "I don't believe that there is any credibility to the notion that the European Union is becoming a military power. The Lisbon Treaty is firmly rooted in the UN Charter in International Law. I believe that the European

Union is mor accurately described as a civilian project."[12]

So our neutrality is not under threat in any way by voting for Lisbon. Our status as the Switzerland of the Atlantic, the Sweden without the good-looking people, the Austria without the decent beer, is intact and unviolated.

TL: Title V, Section 2 TEU

---

12   Mr Blair Horan, Irish Congress of Trade Unions, NFE, 24 April 2008, pg. 43

8 Neutrality #2

We've got the triple-lock provision, that thick rubber prophylactic against sudden military pregnancy.

If there's any deployment of military forces beyond the state's borders, it must be approved by the UN, the Government and the Dáil.

The Treaty does not amend the declaration on Irish neutrality made at the European Council in 2002, formally appended to the Nice Treaty in the 'Seville Declaration'. The No Campaign don't think this is enough. They argue that this leaves it in the hands of the Government and

> If there's any deployment of military forces beyond the state's borders, it must be approved by the UN, the Government and the Dáil.

the Dáil of the day. Hmm. So we can't trust our elected officials to keep their greasy fingers from twisting the tumblers of the triple-locked Irish war machine? Yet if we can't trust our democratically elected government to do our bidding, what are we going to do, give everyone in the country a veto? – Like *everyone*? Even a sandwich-board Messiah who stands for 12-hours-a-day on the median strip of O'Connell Street, dribbling onto his V-neck? Happy now? How about an always exquisitely turned-out old lady who dances along beside him to jazz standards she can hear only in her head?

A policy document called 'A Secure Europe in a Better World' identified five key threats to the security of the EU – terrorism, proliferation of WMD, organised crime, regional conflicts and state failure. None of these can be combatted by purely military means. The EU can bring collective diplomacy to bear in a deployment of 'soft power' to see off such threats. Member states will decide their own military and civilian contributions, but the strength of a collective voice, backed by UN mandate and military deployment if necessary is the way to contain and police cross-border security problems.

And still we have the triple-lock provision to protect us and yes, we have to trust our politicians, as they're the ones we've gone to the bother of electing.

TL: Title V, Section 2 TEU

9 Neutrality #3

Ireland cannot, under Lisbon, join a European Union Common Defence unless and until our Constitutional guarantee is changed by referendum.

The guarantee was introduced into Bunreacht na hÉireann by the referendum on the Nice Treaty in November 2002. The Lisbon Treaty reaffirms this provision.

Ireland is a member of the European Defence Agency along with neutral States such as Sweden, Austria and Finland. The Lisbon Treaty does indeed commit Member States to improve their military capabilities. If we have an army at all, we have to provide them with the personnel, training and equipment to function as the defensive force of a neutral State. This is what we need the army to be, lest we disband it entirely, which has never been the stated aim of any Irish Government. If it exists, it should be part of a European Defence Agency. There is strength in numbers and a small island nation that's had the fun-filled experience of a foreign power defining its borders shouldn't have to learn this lesson twice.

Since the UN features here, let's give that wee rascal Kofi Annan his spake: "I want to leave you in no doubt of how important strengthened EU capacities are to the United Nations. The EU is in a position to provide specialised skills that our greatest troop contributors may not be able to give us and to deploy more rapidly than we can."[13]

When engaging in joint peacekeeping missions with UN and EU forces, it will only work if the Irish army's equipment –

---

13   Ex-UN Secretary-General Kofi Annan, National Forum on Europe, Oct 2004.

guns, transport and communications – is compatible with the other European forces. This will only happen if we are part of the EDA. But this does not mean we have to row into a Common Defence policy unless we vote to by referendum.[14]

The guarantees that all Member States agreed to grant Ireland and that are to become a legally watertight Protocol attached to the next accession Treaty state *'The Treaty of Lisbon does not affect or prejudice Ireland's traditional policy of military neutrality... The Treaty of Lisbon does not provide for the creation of a European army or for conscription to any military formation.'*

100 Reasons asked Roger Cole, chairman of the Peace and Neutrality Alliance (PANA), if he had said he would reverse his position on Lisbon upon the legal guarantees being robust enough.

> A small island nation that's had the fun-filled experience of a foreign power defining its borders shouldn't have to learn this lesson twice.

"What I said was that in the event of a protocol similar to what the Dane s had got, the Danish protocol, not any old protocol, that would exclude Ireland from involving itself in the process of militarisation in Europe, I would recommend to the national executive [PANA] that we accept that and opt out." So, eh, you want the Danish one then, Roger, not the Irish one?

To further clarify matters, he said "If the protocol that was put in wasn't the protocol that was put in, but it was the Danish protocol with the word Denmark changed and Ireland put in, that would

---

14   Yeah, yeah, so we're still talking about neutrality and that's given us a third reason, what can we tell you? We're paid by the reason.

be a different situation." In the event, we got the Irish protocol, not the Danish one, the Irish one, so Roger wasn't budging. Minister for European Affairs Dick Roche responded "The Danes are members of NATO. They carved out that out of Europe, because they express that through NATO. I doubt very much if he'd be very pleased if we decided to join NATO. I wouldn't." The Danish attitude to military action is inherently contradictory.

The Danes have opted out of any part in a EU military involvement whatsoever, which has never been the aim of an Irish Government and thus it's not enough for PANA. Shame really, as they put forward a reasonable argument and were uneasy about being lumped in the No Campaign with Sinn Féin and the now-defunct Libertas. One argument they advance is irrefutable – when a neutral state allows its territory to be used by a foreign power to transport troops to a warzone, all talk of neutrality is faintly ridiculous.

But rest assured, what neutrality we still possess is unassailed by Lisbon.

TL: Title V, Section 2; Article 28D [45] TEU

10 We keep control of our own taxes.

Member States retain their national veto in the field of taxation.

There is no mention in any of the treaties or in Lisbon of direct taxation (esp. corporation tax). Taxation policy remains within the competence and at the discretion of Member States.

MEP Proinsias de Rossa said "...there is nothing to stop any Member State at the moment from reducing its corporation tax to zero if it wants and that will continue to be the position so long as the veto is exercised by Ireland in relation to that issue."[15]

Unanimity at the European Council will still be required for any changes to taxation policy to be made.

"But one thing is already crystal clear – no Member State, either under the current rules or under the Lisbon Treaty, can be obliged to accept a tax proposal to which it objects." Commission President Barroso then said in another debate "nothing can be agreed on taxation issues without Ireland's consent and nothing can be imposed on Ireland."[16] We're also assured by him that the 'distortion of competition' clause is not something that can be set against the unanimity rule for tax matters. It's the Commission President on the record guaranteeing Ireland's right to decide its own taxation policy and levy accordingly. And that's a good thing considering the amount of tax policy jiggery-pokery going on in 2009 to magic up the cash that strangely disappeared into the large fiery pit beneath the IFSC.

15   Proinsias de Rossa MEP, NFE, 6 March 2008 pg. 35
16   José Manuel Barroso, NFE, 17 April 2008 pg. 41; pg 216 Plenary debates.

Fine Gael finance spokesman Richard Bruton says "The irony of this is that the parties who have consistently advocated raising taxes, Sinn Féin and the Socialist Party, are the ones who are telling us apparently that our low tax rates are at risk, whereas the parties who initiated and negotiated the low tax rates that we enjoy are the ones that are giving assurances this will be robust and protected."[17]

> But one thing is already crystal clear – no Member State, either under the current rules or under the Lisbon Treaty, can be obliged to accept a tax proposal to which it objects.

RTE Europe Editor Sean Whelan made the point that Irish tax policy had already been up before the European Court of Justice a number of times and was in some cases found deficient as it was discriminating between Irish and foreign-owned businesses. A recent example was the 2006 Cadburys/Schweppes case where the UK attempted to tax Irish profits arising from multinational groups of companies. In that case, the ECJ ruled in Ireland's favour.

The legal guarantee that Ireland secured from Europe states *Nothing in the Treaty of Lisbon makes any change of any kind, for any member state, to the extent or operation of the competence of the European Union in relation to taxation.*

Ex-MEP Patricia McKenna made the self-defeating point when she talked of the veto we retained on tax issues: "While the veto remains, the one big difference will be that we give our political leaders the right to give away that veto if they so wish

---

at a later date, so what you're talking about is faith in the politicians." Gee, maybe Patricia's right – you just can't trust politicians to do what they've promised they'll do. But, wait, Patricia, aren't you a politician? Doesn't that remind you of a fable about the scorpion and the tortoise crossing a river together? It's in politicians' nature to turn around and sting us in the ass once elected, but what's the alternative? We know they're all power-crazed egomaniacs, but someone's got to wear the poxy suits and saying you can't trust politicians is kind of like saying Colin Farrell likes pussy.

TL: Eh, nowhere, that's the point.

11 There is no dissolution of the ban on abortion by adopting the Lisbon Treaty.

The protocol relating to 40.3.3 in the Irish Constitution on abortion is retained in the Treaty. It states that nothing in the Treaties will affect the operation of 40.3.3 which acknowledges the right to life of the unborn and equally protects the mother's right to life, while not preventing freedom of travel out of the State to obtain an abortion abroad. It also 'does not limit freedom to obtain or make available' information about such services lawfully operating outside the State. Thus we still won't stop young couples in trouble from hopping on the boat to Liverpool, but it sure ain't happening here. What a mature country we are! It's like Clinton's 'Don't Ask, Don't Tell' solution for gay people serving in the US military. It works, but really, it's pretty dumb.

The Protocol states *Nothing in the Treaties or in the Treaty establishing the European Atomic Energy Community or in the Treaties or Acts modifying or supplementing those Treaties, shall affect the application in Ireland of Article 40.3.3 of the Constitution of Ireland.*

Isn't it just a little strange to have the European Atomic Energy Community and the Irish anti-abortion article in the same sentence? Are they trying to hint at something? That the upsurge in abortion in somehow linked to nuclear power? Only if your unborn has twelve heads, a core temperature of 1000 degrees and emits a green glow through your belly, should you consider termination?

The inclusion of the right to life in the first section of the Charter of Fundamental Rights 'Dignity' should also placate the Pro-Life lobby.

In an address to the International Institute of European Affairs, Archbishop Diarmuid Martin stated "We should always remember that in Ireland abortion became legal in certain circumstances not through... Brussels but through an interpretation of the Constitution by an Irish court."[18]

So while COIR's Richard Greene and Niamh Uí Bhrian may yet again accuse the Yes campaign of treason, *100 Reasons* knows that we share no such common feeling with those particular citizens if that's what Irish patriotism has become.[19]

Journalist Stephen Collins writes "spurious concerns such as conscription and the status of abortion have nothing to do with the Treaty."[20] Ah yes, but what about the conscription of the unborn? You haven't thought of that now, Stephen, have you? If by signing the Lisbon Treaty we end up in a military superstate that has no bother with callously slaying the unborn, what's to stop them keeping all the unborn alive, so to speak, thus bearing the unborn, making them born and growing them into SuperEuroKillingMachines in giant Strasbourg incubator farms?

This re-affirmation in the Protocol – that nothing affects Ireland's constitutional ban on abortion – is also included in the legal guarantees granted to Ireland in June in the 'Right to Life, Family and Education Section', which themselves will become a Protocol. So the legally-binding rule appears in two separate Protocols, like a clink-while-you-walk chastity belt double-padlocked and wrapped in prickly barbed wire.

TL: Protocol on Article 40.3.3 of the Constitution of Ireland

18   Archbishop Martin, IIEA, 3 March 2008
19   *Irish Independent*, 21 Nov. 2008
20   Stephen Collins, *The Irish Times*, 7 Feb. 2008

12 Protects the environment and promotes energy security

The Treaty includes 'combating climate change' and promoting 'energy security' as stated objectives of the EU for the first time.

"The Lisbon Treaty will make it easier for the EU to make policy in areas that the public wants us to intervene; like climate change and energy security. For the first time, these will explicitly become matters of EU responsibility. EU countries will be able to get their collective act together in cutting greenhouse gas emissions, in talking with one voice to Russia and to other suppliers of gas and oil."[21] Ms. Margot Wallstrom, who as Environment Commissioner negotiated the Kyoto protocol, also said that the European Union had already 'set the standards for the rest of the world.'

A lot of EU laws press its members into accepting and then enforcing new standards of environmental protection. The EU countries have more weight negotiating as one on issues like this with industrialised, fossil fuel-burning nations such as the United States. This is one area where it is abundantly clear that the competence is fully with the EU and fully justified in being so.

Green Party senator Deirdre de Burca highlights that "The Charter of Fundamental Rights attached to the Lisbon Treaty states that a high level of environmental protection and the improvement of the quality of the environment must be integrated into the policies of the Union. Furthermore, Article 191 of the Lisbon Treaty commits the EU to promoting measures at an international level to deal with regional or world-

---

21   Ms. Margot Wallstrom, Vice-President of the Commission, NFE, 28 Feb. 2008, pg. 9

wide environmental problems, and in particular combating climate change."[22]

Promoting energy efficiency, the development of renewable energy and ensuring the security of energy supply in the EU is of the greatest importance. This doesn't affect Member States' competence in choosing what energy sources to use and how it organises its energy supply.

The EU have already learned lessons from the gas supply crisis this year sparked by the Ruskies turning off the pipes to Ukraine. On January 1st, Ukraine rejected a gas price hike from $50 to $230 (per 1000 cubic metres on average) and Moscow abruptly stopped the supply in response. France, Poland and Italy all use the Ukraine's pipeline, so their gas supplies plummeted in the middle of a harsh winter. Eventually a five-year compromise price deal was hammered out. A quarter of Western Europe's gas still comes from Russia and there are plans to source a even greater proportion from there, so we are vulnerable to such bullying tactics. Gazprom, the Russian monopoly gas and oil producer, is the largest producer of gas and oil in the world. It's quite terrifying to consider that the Gazprom is 51% state-owned and that the Russian President Medvedev is the ex-Chairman of the Board of Directors, a role he retained when he was Deputy Prime Minister. Maybe Brian Cowen would inspire

> Maybe Brian Cowen would inspire more fear in his political enemies if he wasn't just the landlord to student accommodation in Leeds and instead all-powerful controller of world energy

---

22   Senator Deirdre de Búrca, NFE, 18 Feb. 2008, pg. 55

more fear in his political enemies if he wasn't just the landlord to student accommodation in Leeds and instead all-powerful controller of world energy. There'd be no paunchy portraits of him popping up in the National Gallery then. He'd have his own secret police plucked from the ranks of loyal Offaly hurlers ready to knock some heads.

The Russia/Ukraine flare-up has got the Energy Commissioner thinking about diversification. The Commission has brokered a deal between four EU states, Hungary, Romania, Bulgaria and Austria to team up with Turkey on the Nabucco pipeline that will yearly deliver up to 31 billion cubic metres of Caspian gas 3,300km via Turkey thus easing the reliance on imported Russian natural gas.[23]

TL: Article 174 [191], 176A [194] TFEU

---

23   BBC website 13 July 2009

13 Finally, a space policy of our own

The Treaty calls for the drafting of a European Space Policy. If the Russians sent up dogs, what animal would best represent the EU in space? With all the talk of CAP reform, the animal most representative of the EU is probably the cow. An Australian or African space agency could send up some pretty wacky animals to keep the extra-terrestrials guessing, but we'd probably have to plump for intergalactic friesians cunningly hidden Russian doll-like in Gateway computer boxes.

Rather worryingly though, it goes on to say *the Union shall establish any appropriate relations with the European Space Agency*. So that's not us then? Alright, strike that. Call back the space cattle. That's just embarrassing. The EU wants a space policy, but there's already a European Space Agency, but they're kinda crap. While you've heard of them, they haven't exactly been troubling NASA for supremacy up there in the great black void. So they could probably use the help, or we need to take it over. That's why this narrowly qualifies as a reason you should vote Yes.

When you are about halfway through reading the Treaty and tiny droplets of blood are dripping from your eyes onto the page, you might start to think that a lot of this brotherhood-of-man stuff and protection of illegal aliens sounds a bit *Star Trek* and now you know why. In March this year, there was a UN 'Creative Community Outreach' conference held in Washington centred on the diplomatic lessons that could be learned by politicians from the storylines of *Battlestar Galactica*[24] – if you combined this with the University of Limerick symposium on the lyrics of Morrissey in April, you'd

---

24   I shit you not.

actually have an EU thinktank with maudlin / sci-fi entertainment value. If only Morrissey had gone space-age glam (apart from the grey stripe in his fringe), it'd work. You'd have to give Major Tom a shout and see if the original Man who fell to Earth and his Spiders from Mars were available for guest lecture spots.

Right now, the sort of cutting edge training the ESA offer prospective spacemen is locking them in a small capsule for 105 days, with half-hour delays on e-mail and text messages to see if they'll go fruit loop with boredom and claustrophobia. With the low quality of broadband infrastructure and rising unemployment here, that qualifies a lot of Irish people to be Euronauts. That's something to consider for the next FÁS form. This is the *Mars 500* experiment going on in Moscow (see? They have to ask the Russians for help, even with this!). They've locked five dudes – three Ruskies, a German and a Frenchmen – in a tin can for 105 days to see exactly how unhappy they get in preparation for a bigger experiment of locking them in for 500 days to mimic the eighteen months it would take for a manned mission to Mars. Imagine *Big Brother* without the sunlight, playpool and George Galloway on all-fours mewling like a cat.

You won't be able to locate any articles in the Treaty that deal with what to say when you encounter non-humanoid alternative life forms. Instead our Euronauts are just going to have to wing it by offering them croissants, strong Turkish ciggies (they'll be in by then) and a rather large dose of diplomatic immunity from any meddling the US Military might have in store for our new, blue (with yellow star-like splotches) friends and hope for the best. If that doesn't curry favour, they'd have to go for broke and hand over the Hungarian porn. Our first EU Alien. Now that really will be a brave new world.

TL: Article 172A [189] TFEU

14 Protects human rights #1

Lisbon greatly enhances human rights and freedoms with the incorporation of the Charter of Fundamental Rights.

It gives the Charter the same legal force as the Treaties. Thus the bar is raised for enlargement. Turkey and Croatia must clean their houses before they'll be cleared for entry. The Charter provides that *'everyone whose rights and freedoms guaranteed by the law of the Union are violated has the right to an effective remedy before a tribunal...'* The content of the Charter of Fundamental Rights is broader than that of the 1950 European Convention for the Protection of Human Rights and Fundamental Freedoms (ECHR), including the right to life, education, equality before the law, freedom of thought and to workers' rights, such as collective action and collective bargaining. It's organised into seven sections: Dignity, Freedoms, Equality, Solidarity, Citizen's rights, Justice and General Provisions. The Union accedes to the ECHR in the same article.

John Monks, General Secretary of the European Trade Union Confederation has said "it was a step forward compared to existing provisions, for example in relation to the legal enforcement of the Charter of Fundamental Rights, commitments to full employment, the social market economy, and public services."[25]

Michael D. Higgins told us "The Lisbon Treaty speaks of a 'social market economy.' In that phrase I believe we can see two very different conceptions of the economy - that of the Left and that of the Right. I believe in the social economy, where

---

25   Speech to Irish Congress of Trade Unions, 10 July 2009

the economy serves the people whereas others believe in the market economy, where the people serve the economy. The two are enshrined in the Treaty cementing the contest between the Left and Right. In the arsenal of the Left, the Charter will be fundamental to our efforts for building of an economy for the people of our country."

Dick Roche loves the Charter – he finds the language used in it uplifting – his enthusiasm for it is positively infectious and when he spoke to *100 Reasons* in Iveagh House, he was practically bouncing Tigger-like (but not Tom Cruise-like) on the couch. He enthused "The constitutional prohibition that you would ever have slavery seems a little odd, but it doesn't exist in Bunreacht na hÉireann." Now let's be clear - he didn't mean that it was odd it should be there at all. He wasn't saying he was relieved it wasn't in Bunreacht na hÉireann. *100 Reasons* is reliably informed that Dick has long since sacked all his slaves and renewed their contracts incorporating all the provisions of the Charter.

Members of the No Campaign including socialist MEP Joe Higgins maintain that there is nothing new in the Charter and it doesn't improve workers' rights. It is true that the rights listed are derived from the Union's Treaties and related case law, existing international conventions like the ECHR or from the common constitutional traditions of the Member States. Yet now they are given legal status and must be brought to bear when drafting every EU proposal.

"...once the Charter becomes legally binding, every single policy, decision, regulation and directive which has the potential to affect an Irish citizen which comes from an EU institution has to comply with the Charter."[26]

---

26   Una McGurk, Alliance for Europe, Pat Kenny Show, RTE Radio 1, 9 June 2008

Not only that, but all Member States must also fully comply with the Charter when implementing any EU law. Former Fine Gael MEP John Cushnahan asked Joe Higgins in a Forum debate, "If the Charter was so worthless, why was it resisted by the British and Polish Governments?"[27] The Government did not seek to join the British/Polish Protocol that seeks to clarify the application of the Charter with regard to their national laws.

While it was all well and good to proclaim the Charter at Nice, the Lisbon Treaty actually gives it legal force and consolidates all the rights in one document making it more visibly a powerful weapon in protecting human rights across the EU.

MEP Proinsias de Rossa weighed in with "The Charter challenges the neo-liberal project, now in deep crisis, in a fundamental way. It puts citizens' rights at the heart of the European project and copper fastens the Lisbon Treaty commitment to a social-market economy."

TL: Article 6 TEU; Protocol on the application of the Charter of Fundamental Rights of the European Union to Poland and to the United Kingdom (no. 30)

---

27   John Cushnahan, NFE, 15 May 2008

15 Greater public scrutiny of the Council of Ministers

Council of Ministers meetings would be conducted in public when enacting new EU policies or legislation.

This hopefully will usher in the end of the portrayal of Brussels as a beast divorced from its Member countries, when the national ministers can be observed by their own citizens walking the tightrope between serving national interests and moving Europe-wide policies forward.

Like *Oireachtas Report*, it'll be another graveyard televisual highlight treasured by nighthawk security guards, insomniacs, political bloggers like Guido Fawkes and, well, politician's wives (and husbands) checking that their other halves didn't go on the mitch/how that tie looked under the green fluorescent lights/does the new haircut give him or her added gravitas? It's nice to know it's there, but don't expect any YouTube gold like the all-out brawl in the Mexican parliament.

It's an encouraging development because of an added layer of transparency that decreases the democratic deficit and bridges the territorial cleavage between citizens and Brussels. Yada, yada, yada... snooze.

Look it, we can see them, the little expense account gougers, whinging away on our behalf. It's a good thing, as once they're jumping through hoops in your living room, you own them. Soap stars and now politicians. The glorious onward march of progress!

TL: Article 16A [15] TFEU

16 Gives EU citizens the chance to affect EU policy directly

Lisbon provides for the citizens' initiative, where ordinary citizens can petition the EU on any policy matter.

The citizens' initiative is a device whereby EU citizens can challenge the institutions by gathering together a petition of over a million signatures to invite the European Commission to submit a proposal on any matter where the citizens want legislation. The Commission is obliged under the rumbling of a million marching feet or, more likely, a million tapping index fingers to consider the proposal.

Barrosso described it thus: "There will also be a possibility for 'people power' - if I may use the word (sic) – in the form of a citizens' initiative whereby one million people across Europe can ask the Commission to take action in areas of concern to them."[28]

> The Citizen's Initiative is a fun-filled way of meeting foreign totty online while appearing deep and politically-engaged.

A million signatures out of 500 million in the age of the internet petition is not a difficult number to muster, but it is a significant enough number of EU citizenry to hopefully frustrate the more crackpot proposals. After Obama made so many US citizens feel and indeed know that they had been directly instrumental in putting him in the White House beyond just the casting of their votes, but also through a highly savvy internet information and fun-

---

28   Barroso, 17 April, 2008, Plenary Debates, pg. 216

draising campaign, this is a patently achievable number to activate this tool for communicating pressing issues directly to the Commission.

How about a petition proposing a political/cultural/psycho-sexual Union and homeland for all Celtic Druids scattered throughout the Shetland isles, Galway, Brittany and Dorset? Think of it as Israel for crusties. That initiative would hopefully start faltering around the 50,000 mark. How many Euro-idiots do you think there are? Look at Facebook, you say? Hmm, this could be a problem.

So there you have it, the Citizen's Initiative is a fun-filled way of meeting foreign totty online while appearing deep and politically-engaged.

TL: Article 8B [11] TEU; Article 21 [24] TFEU

17 Enhances co-operation between EU members

Acts adopted in the framework of enhanced co-operation shall bind only participating Member States.

Enhanced co-operation is a set of arrangements where some, but not all Member States want to co-operate more closely. Now generally it is wise to be wary of anything that proclaims itself 'enhanced' or promises 'enhancement.' Penis enhancement, for instance, sounds a whole lot better than 'severing of the suspensory ligament, suspending weights off the gland, animal fat injection and dermal-matrix grafts'. All this and the risk of impotence and having a Franken-penis that looks like a lumpy prizefighter run to fat. Enhanced interrogation is another lovely little euphemism that the writer sincerely prays he is never on the wrong side of, exhausted, gasping for breath, spurting blood, electrodes hanging from his non-enhanced genitalia.

So with due caution we proceed to enhanced co-operation. It's more like a 'special friendship.' (And no, that's not a euphemism either.)

Such co-operation shall be open at any time to all Member States. This facility is still looked on as one of last resort, as it is preferable for all Union States to go ahead with policies unanimously and as a whole organisation. All Member States are still present when the policies being dealt with by enhanced co-operation are discussed and take part in the deliberations, but only those joining in are entitled to a vote. This sounds perfectly equitable.

Ireland, along with the UK, pursues its policy of 'semi-detachment' from all Title V areas (External Actions and Common

Foreign and Security Policy) and that's fine. When it relates to any proposals under the rubric of common foreign and security policy, it must be approved by the Council acting unanimously. This request goes straight to the High Rep who gives his/her opinion on whether the proposal is consistent with Union foreign policy and the Commission decides on whether it's consistent with other Union policies and then the Council votes on it - only those Member States participating in enhanced co-operation may actually vote. When it relates to the other policy areas, the request goes to the Commission.

Any enhanced co-operation shall respect the competences, rights and obligations of those Member States which do not participate in it. Those Member States shall not impede its implementation by the participating Member States.

To those who proclaim this as the start of a two-tier Europe, why not? They can take the high road and we'll tootle along the low road waiting for the chance to cut up across the grass verge to the high road once it suits us. Enhanced co-operation is open, at the start and later, to all Member States.

Any enhanced co-operation arrangements of course cannot undermine the internal market or act as *a barrier to or discrimination in trade between Member States, nor shall it distort competition between them.*

So these checks and balances make sure this is a way to increase efficiency, without forcing legislation on Member States who want to pursue an independent path in a particular policy area.

TL: 10 [20] TEU; 280 [326-34] TFEU

18 Allows the EU to provide centrally coordinated humanitarian assistance.

The Treaty establishes a European Voluntary Humanitarian Aid Corps to provide ad hoc assistance to victims of man-made or natural disasters.

Let's hope that this minimises the chances of the EU having a Katrina-like catastrophe on its conscience.

With massive humanitarian disasters coming out of freak weather events with a disturbing degree of regularity, this is a strand of EU policy that needs to be separate from any responses drawing on military resources.

Budgets, equipment and personnel specifically need to be set aside prepared to respond to these horrific occurrences as soon as they happen. To institutionalise this paternal response of goodwill from the European people seems both practical and in keeping with the tenets which underpin the community from the start.

The Treaty states *Humanitarian aid operations shall be conducted in compliance with the principles of international law and with the principles of impartiality, neutrality and non-discrimination.*

Now *100 Reasons* can't make a joke about this one – disasters are no laughing matter. They're just not nice at all, to watch on telly, to read about in the paper and most especially, if your house has just been ripped apart by a raging cyclone, you're hanging onto a tree and you can't see the church spire anymore. Although I suppose George Bush made a joke out of the people of New Orleans when the US Government response was at best derisory and at worst callous, leading rapper Kanye West to say that 'George Bush doesn't care about black people.' Let's hope that this minimises the chances of the EU having a Katrina-like catastrophe on its conscience.

TL: Article 188J [214] TFEU

19 National sovereignty is strengthened.

An exit clause provides procedures for Member States wishing to leave the EU.

Article 50 outlines the divorce procedures if a Member State wants to withdraw. It's really about setting up the rules by which this anti-social, maverick, loner State is going to inter-act with the 24-hour Euro-party in the future. If the loner State wants to sit in and read an improving novel, but Euro-party's making too much noise and having way too much fun next door, how many bangs on the wall are appropriate to get the music (techno, sorry – the Germans) turned down? That sort of thing.

The Member State in question cannot engage in the separa-tion negotiations at the Council. Watch, but don't speak. It's as close as anyone will get to attending their own funeral. It gets to see who nabs the Simply Red CD, the cat, the bonzai tree and the list of what mutual friendly countries it's still allowed to meet up with. The State has to set out *a framework for its future relationship with the Union.* They then either set a date for when the Treaties no longer apply to that country, or it occurs automatically two years after first notification of the wish to skedaddle.

If however, the loner State gets sick of Friday nights in alone reading Tolstoy, engaging in energetic acts of onanism and eating pasta spirals 'n' tuna (because what's the point in cook-ing a proper meal, when it's just for one?) and wants back into the party, then it has to prove itself worthy once more. A comb must be dragged through the greasy hair, deodorant applied and it has to present itself at the Euro-party door bearing a full bag of Dutch Gold and a sheepish smile. It must then jump through the same hoops as the brand-spanking-new applicant countries and prove itself a suitably entertaining guest who's not just going to swipe all the booze from the fridge, while hiding its naggin of vodka behind the sofa.

> Watch, but don't speak. It's as close as anyone will get to attending their own funeral.

It's also a good argument for voting Yes to Lisbon if you want to see Ireland leave the European project completely. Vote Yes and then spearhead a campaign for Ireland to withdraw from the EU – *100 Reasons* is sure that's the one that'll capture the public imagination.

TL: Article 49A [50] TEU

20 The scope of legal redress for European citizens is widened.

The entire area of Justice and Home affairs will be brought under the jurisdiction of the European Court of Justice (ECJ), with the deletion of Article 46.

The ECJ rules on actions brought by Member States, institutions or by ordinary citizens like us (and we're presuming, but we can't be too careful, like you). You see? We're being *legalistic* and *prudent* in the deployment of any of our assumptions (which we all know have the ever present possibility of backfiring and making an ass of u and mptions.)

It acts as the referee settling disagreements, beefs, barneys and/or, but not excluding contretemps between Member States, between the EU and Member States, as well as between the institutions and between EU citizens.

They give preliminary rulings at the request of courts or tribunals of Member States, which is good, because we have a lot of those and they interpret Union law, which is all about the feel, the nuance, the delicate give and resonance of a particular piece of incomprehensible guff in the context of a very long tract that plays fast 'n' loose with normal rules of punctuation, ignores clauses altogether and then ends abrup.

The Court of Justice shall continue to consist of one judge from each Member State. It is assisted by Advocates-General. The Court of Justice of the European Union does not however have jurisdiction with respect to Common Foreign and Security Policy.

The judges of the ECJ and the General Court are appointed by common accord of the governments of the Member States for a period of six years. Retiring judges and Advocates-General can be re-appointed. Only candidates whose *independence is beyond doubt* will be appointed. That would be the non-judgmental judges then. Wise men and distinguished grey ladies who know whether there's an 'e' in judg(e)mental in any language: they're the type of sage, down-to-earth high-fliers the Council's going to be gunning for.

Wise men and distinguished grey ladies who know whether there's an e in judg(e)mental in any language.

What's worrying though is the capacity for confusion depending on which language Treaty the judges are reading. Maybe they tend to do it in English or French or German, but the Treaty has equal legal standing in Czech, Bulgarian, Danish, Dutch, Estonian, Finnish, Portuguese, Greek, Slovak, Slovenian, Swedish, Lithuanian, Polish, Maltese, Hungarian, Romanian, Italian, Latvian, Spanish and *Irish*. We should send them a Gaelgeoir judge – now that's Court TV people would watch. When a fair portion of a Council meeting was engaged on deciding what the word 'Euro' should be in Bulgarian (true), I think this might be a problem...

TL: 9F [19] TEU

21 Lisbon will not turn the EU into a superstate.

A measure of how much power has been ceded to the EU can be seen in monetary terms – the EU budget constitutes only 2% of the Member States' public expenditure. So if we have ceded all our power to a European Superstate, we haven't ceded much of our cash to it. Always follow the money. It's as good a gauge of how much sovereignty we've given to the European Project and it's tiny. It's astounding how much can get done from goodwill, co-operation and a fraction of your yearly budget.

Moravcsik argues that 'the EU is now pre-eminent in trade, agriculture, fishing, Eurozone monetary policy and some business regulation and helps coordinate cooperation in foreign policy.'[29] This corresponds to about 20 per cent of legislation and as this is how the division of competences has evolved, there is no political will to deepen integration.

€133.8 billion is the 2009 EU Budget. Duties on imports from non-EU countries comes to roughly 15% of total income. Then a uniform percentage rate of 0.73% is applied to the Gross National Income of each Member State. Although it is a balancing item, it has become the largest source of revenue and today accounts for 69% of total revenue or €80 billion. The proportion of the budget that isn't spent is usually tiny, as in 2008 at 1.5% and these funds are returned to the Member states, with Ireland getting €23.6 million back in coppers.[30] When we're contributing 50 per cent of our public expenditure to the EU, then we can worry.

TL: There ain't no superstate clause.

---

29   Laffan, B, in Brown, T. *What the Reform Treaty Means*, pg. 61
30   European Commission website, ec.europa.eu

22 Better balance of power between the Commission and the Parliament

The Commission's role and power has been diluted by the introduction of the 'co-decision' procedure sharing legislative power between the European Parliament, the Council and the Council of Ministers.

The Commission presents a proposal to the European Parliament which adopts its 'position at first reading' and passes it on to the Council. If the Council is happy with the wording, it can adopt it at this stage and send it back to the EP. If the Council is not happy with the Parliament's position, it will adopt its own 'position at first reading'.

There is a three-month deadline for the EP to respond with a position of second reading. The proposals go back and forth between the Council and Parliament through this second and perhaps third reading, until all amendments have been appended to ensure agreement and the passing of the legislation. After the second reading, if agreement hasn't been reached, a conciliation committee made up equally of Council and Parliament members is convened and they vote by qualified majority on a joint text. If they can't agree on a joint text within six weeks, it goes to a third reading.

The Commission is sent each new version and asked for its opinion on each of these. Like college essays, there is of course provision made for time extensions (one month on top of three months and a measly two weeks on top of the six weeks) for these processes, but the deadlines (also like college essays, or indeed any written work, including this one) are there to encourage swift progress or at least some progress, or maybe some faint grey hope of thinking about maybe getting down to progress once they've had a nap, four cups of tea, watched two episodes of *The Wire* and then clipped their toenails.

It's the Council, the Parliament and the Council of Ministers who are involved in the co-decision mechanism.

It's clear though that while the Commissioner with the back-up of civil servants research and draft the proposals, it's the Council, the Parliament and the Council of Ministers who are involved in the co-decision mechanism.

TL: Article 251 [294] TFEU

23 Improves mutual emergency assistance for member states

The Solidarity clause provides for a joint response between the EU and Member States to a terrorist attack or manmade/natural disaster.

This article gives discretion as to what level of assistance each Member State actually gives. This gives us a level of protection in numbers should a Madrid-scale attack or a large-scale natural disaster occur here.

Happily for us, there are no volcanoes in the Cooley Peninsula and an earthquake is unlikely to dunk Cobh into the sea, but considering the continued use of Shannon airport as a refuelling point for US troops, Ireland is a legitimate al-Qaeda target, 'neutrality' intact or no. When *100 Reasons* put this to Dick Roche, he didn't like it very much, but he did say "When Belfast was bombed during the war, the first instinct for Eamon De Valera was to send the ambulance and the civil defence North. That was a breach of the rules of neutrality. But he said to hell, our people are dying and they need our help." With this he was referring to the moral underpinnings of the solidarity clause and not the State's facilitation of the US military. The EU was helpful in assisting the State deal with the terrorist threat in the North and we may yet need its help in quashing ongoing dissident Republican activity. You just never know. And it's nice to have a 'you just never know' clause.

Our peace-loving Galwegian poet politician Michael D. Higgins joked "this clause absolutely and totally does not mean that our children or citizens will be required to fight in Poland's; Britain's; or even Malta's army. The Rangers will not be expected to don warm, white, padded clothing and patrol Finland's borders, gingerly stepping over concealed landmines." Our fears of military manoeuvres charted in advance by rolling Maltesers across the map or of playing footsie with incendiary Finnish snowballs are thus assuaged.

Of course, if a dirty bomb goes off on Dublin's Dame street, it doesn't give the EU the right to take over the response on the ground, as the political authorities of the attacked country must request the EU's assistance. The Political and Security Commitee would co-operate with a standing committee on Internal Security that's established with Lisbon to coordinate the Union's actions should such an attack take place followed by a Member State's cry for help.

TL: *Article 188R [222] TFEU*

24 Lisbon consolidates the Union.

If and when Lisbon is ratified, it'll mean the end of this institutional evolution and give the EU a chance to stabilise and concentrate on the issues at hand for a change. It's more than overdue to focus attention and action on policy delivery and to leave institutional arguments to the historians.

"Failure to ratify would thrust the EU as a whole back into the introspection of the 'period of reflection', when what is clearly needed is an end, for the foreseeable future, to the institutional debates that have dragged on for almost a decade, confusing and alienating public opinion."[31]

Labour leader Eamon Gilmore makes this reasoned argument and then Chancellor Angela Merkel adopts the tone of a strict nanny: 'Stop this navel gazing and stop simply talking about institutions. We have done that. We have had enough of that.'[32]

Nanny-tone or not, you can understand the impatience bordering on exasperation. Lisbon has been seven years in the making and for anyone to pretend that the EU Institutional reforms have in any way been rushed or we're being bamboozled by shotgun legislation, is lying through their teeth.

The alarm clock of global economic and environmental doom is chiming. Do we want to spend another five years bickering about the structures? We surely neither have nor need that luxury.

TL: the whole thing.

---

31   Eamon Gilmore, Plenary sessions pg. 37
32   Angela Merkel, 92nd Plenary session, 14 April 2008, pg.199

25 For the money

To date, Ireland has received €62 billion in European Fund Transfers since 1973. Two thirds of this relates to agriculture. The European Social Fund and European Regional Development Fund account for some 10% and 13% respectively. With payments from us of over €21 billion to the EU budget, this makes Ireland a net recipient of nearly €41 billion.[33]

This accounting allocation, among other drawbacks, is non-exhaustive and gives no indication whatsoever of many of the other benefits gained from EU policies such as economic integration, political stability, security and the internal market – for example, what would be the cost to Irish exporters if they had to comply with twenty-seven different national regulations if there were no single market?

Do you remember the days when you could tell the exact point you'd crossed the border to the North, as the quality of the roads jumped up in standard? The sound under the wheels would change from spitting gravel and thundering potholes to an eerie smooth, calm flat that one would associate with soldiers and bombscares and the Buttercrane Shopping Centre. Now the difference between North and South is negligible. EU Structural Funds kickstarted the modernisation of the country and then were backed up by exchequer investment, even though it's clear now that Ireland didn't invest enough in its own basic infrastructure during the boom.

Now it's dubious to believe in the concept of Catholic guilt – having one's afternoon delight spoiled by thoughts of 'what would Jesus do?' accompanied by the music from the *Godfather*. But

33   European Commission website ec.europa.eu

financial guilt? Everyone experiences that on perusal of their monthly credit card statement. The Structural Funds are part of the Union's regional and social policies that assist those economies that are lagging behind to catch up. We caught up certainly, but we didn't do it alone by pulling on our mucky bootstraps.

Now it's entirely possible, as journalist Mark Hennessy believes, that we were made the EU's pet to show Britain just what it was missing.[34] Showing the world that a English-speaking territory at the edge of Europe would not become a de facto US State might have been another motive. Whatever the cause, we were indulged and like any spoilt child, we too soon decided our small, open, market economy didn't need EU Sugar Daddy anymore, sure didn't we have Uncle Sam looking after us, too? With the glory days of Foreign Direct Investment by US companies now abruptly over on the back of protectionist pressures, spiralling Irish wage costs, high overheads and a worldwide depression, we need to reconsider our attitude to Europe and what being an integral part of it can offer us and what, of course, we can offer it. But never underestimate the goodwill deficit, as those billions can be easily transformed into a stick to beat us with by the German taxpayers who funded it.

However it's not simple altruism on behalf of the stronger countries of Europe – if you support poorer economies, it will bring them up to your level and create new markets for your exports. Now while we're still net beneficiaries of EU funding, despite our per capita GDP being for the past number of years at the higher end of the EU average, this was not undertaken for any other reason by the Union other than that it makes sound business sense. Still, the guilt does be killin' us.

TL: Eh, no guilt section, apart from in between the lines.

---

34   Mark Hennessy, *The Irish Times*, 17 February 2009

26 Lisbon protects asylum seekers.

The Lisbon Treaty has introduced a specific reference to compliance with the principle of non-refoulement.

This means nobody can be returned to a place where their life is threatened.

This means nobody can be returned to a place where their life is threatened, like outside a Dundalk chipper or where they face a threat of persecution, like Louth in general. This falls within the common policy on asylum, subsidiary protection and temporary protection.

The common policy would also have to comply with the Geneva Convention relating to the status of refugees. The benefit of having a common asylum policy across the EU cannot be overstated. However this doesn't stop Member States from setting admission volumes for third-country nationals.

It is not a policy that has anything to do with dirty chickens, it's not about that at all.

TL Article 63 [78] TFEU

27 The EU shall have legal personality.

This will allow the Union itself to take legal action, to become a member of international organisations like the UN and to be part of an international convention.

It also allows it to sign and ratify international treaties like the European Convention on Human Rights, as it confers on the Union the ability to enter into a contract. It makes the EU more effective, certain and legally transparent.

A personality. What a personality that young fella is! When referring to young children, it's got something to do with strong will, sense of fun and sheer God-given charisma. When referring to public figures, a personality must be a celebrity who can actually talk, thus ruling out 50 Cent, because he got shot in the mouth. When referring to a loose union of sovereign nations, it just means this blue & yellow vat of pooled resources, as Fiddy might say if he could, has got game.

Not only has the EU legal personality got game, it's a proud, card-carrying representative of all its members' interests on the world stage. It's got the imprimatur from the Irish and everyone else to act in areas where a strong collective voice might just steer us all clear of difficulties with the US, China, multinationals and those damn annoying international terrorists. And it needs all the charisma it can get to deal with that lot.

TL: Article 46A [47] TEU

28 Gives smaller member states better levels of representation

In the European Parliament, representation will be broadly in proportion to population, but with more favourable treatment for the smaller Member States.

This can only serve to increase Ireland's ability to make itself heard. The number of MEPs is capped at 750 (it was 732 under Nice, then readjusted up to 736), plus the Parliament's President, who also has a vote, as otherwise he or she would have a wee cry – that's not a cry where you cry and wee at the same time, just an innocent Northernism. In the transitional Parliament from 2009 to 2014, there'll be 754 in the Parliament, with Germany set to lose three MEPs in 2014, bringing it down to the maximum allowed.

> For Ireland, that's one seat per 358,000 people, while it's 854,000 Germans per seat.

There's a minimum of six and a maximum of ninety-six MEPs per country. It's nicely skewed in favour of the smaller nations. For the 2009 elections here, Ireland has 12 seats, the same as was agreed under Nice. Germany, for instance, gets the maximum of 96 MEPs. For Ireland, that's one seat per 358,000 people, while it's 854,000 Germans per seat. That's got to be hard to swallow for the Gunthers, Sabines and Wolfgangs out there, but we're not complaining about this aspect of the EU structure.[35]

TL: 190 [223] TFEU

---

35   David Byrne, Former EU Commissioner, 91st session, NFE, April 10 2008

29 Ensures protection for workers, public services and competition

The European Trade Union Confederation insisted that seven key social issues originally covered by the Constitutional Treaty would have to be retained in the new Treaty:

(1) the values and principles set out in the Constitutional Treaty
(2) references to full employment and the social market economy
(3) recognition of the role of the social partners
(4) the Charter of Fundamental Rights, with legal force
(5) the citizens initiative
(6) the legal base for services of general interest
(7) the Social Clause

If none of these clauses have any worth, why would the European trade unionists fight so hard to retain them? This would imply that the 'Third Way' between socialism and capitalism is not dead yet and that it's possible to pursue 'competition without distortion' and yet ensure that workers' rights are upheld and the Social Partners are involved in negotiation on public policy. The Treaty does not extend the competition provisions into public services. Protocol 16 does not endanger that. It specifically does not extend competition into 'health and education' services, so shopping around your various private primary school providers isn't going to happen on the basis of Lisbon.

It's unlikely that the trade union organisations of Europe can ever go back to the era of 'beer and sandwiches' where communication and co-operation with the employers was routine, certainly after the steady erosion of their clout since the outright defeats of the eighties. However, if social protection can go along with the right to seek work anywhere in the Union, then we're still on the right track. Hmm, beer and sandwiches – that sounded like a lovely time. A time before managers in France and Spain were kidnapped and offices trashed by incensed ex-workers, a time before workers at Continental piled up the tyres and set them alight. Just think of a time when men could wear moustaches without irony, or as an indication of sexual preference and actually competed as to whose didn't join up properly in the middle. A time when you could roll your sleeves up over your tattooed forearms and smoke unfiltered cigarettes before lunch, after lunch, during lunch, in the canteen, in the canteen's kitchen, on the cycle home, in the car, in the pub, but not on the couch, because the wife didn't like it. Health and Safety just wouldn't allow it anymore.

> If none of these clauses have any worth, why would the European trade unionists fight so hard to retain them?

"All the social policy content as well as the key demands of the Social Platform group of NGOs that were successfully negotiated by the European Convention into the Constitution, is carried over into the Lisbon Treaty, including the new legal base for the protection of public services."[36]

The Head of the ETUC John Monks told us that "There's no conditions: we want the Lisbon Treaty through. We want that Charter of Fundamental Rights."

TL: throughout

---

36 Mr Proinsias De Rossa MEP, Plenary debates, NFE, 5 February 2008, pg. 53

30 Allows the EU to expand... cautiously

The 'Copenhagen criteria' or conditions of eligibility for applicant countries come into effect with the Lisbon Treaty.

The try-out State has to demonstrate the stability

> It's like a talent show for countries...

of its institutions guaranteeing democracy, the rule of law, human rights and protection of minorities. It has to prove it has a functioning market economy and the ability to cope with absorption into the Common Market. Above all, it has to show its willingness to take on the obligations of membership, which includes adherence to the aims of political, economic and monetary union.

It's like a talent show for countries – if you can show that you like money as much as the other States, but you don't like money so much that you're willing to harbour vicious international crime organisations, that your financial institutions are (miraculously) less corrupt and generally bolloxed than the ones in another EU Member of 'good standing' (let's say, Ireland) then you'll be free to pull on your one-piece swimsuit and pumps and totter down the ramp for the Council to get a good look at those child-bearing haunches of yours.

If however, you still like locking up your native citizens in secret dungeons for having the temerity to write 'allegories' that could be viewed as perhaps a bit snippy towards the administration, well then it'll be a while yet before you get to wrap yourself in the EU colours at a Boulevard cafe while delicately holding your espresso cup with your pinkie finger raised in the foppish Euro-fashion.

The applicant countries must adhere to the principles of the EU which state *the Union is founded on the values of respect for human dignity, freedom, democracy, equality, the rule of law and respect for human rights, including the rights of persons belonging to minorities. These values are common to the Member States in a society in which pluralism, non-discrimination, tolerance, justice, solidarity and equality between women and men prevail.*

The Copenhagen criteria taken in conjunction with the Charter of Fundamental Rights further raise the bar for Turkey and Croatia.

TL: 1A [2]; Article 49 TEU

31 Lisbon won't lead to increased militarism.

The ratification of the Lisbon Treaty won't create a new 'arms race' with the United States.

Pat Cox quotes figures published by the independent watchdog Stockholm International Peace Research Institute to make the point that US defence spending is 2.9 times larger than the entire EU budget.[37]

The entire European Union spending on external policy is just under 2 per cent of the United States' defence spending in 2007. The 2007 Defence and Armaments Budget of the US (coming in unsurprisingly at world No.1) was €582.7 billion. 5.7% of the EU budget is spent on the EU as global actor which amounts to €7.3 billion. This is the equivalent of 2% of the defence budget of the United States.

> Even with the least bellicose US President in decades, the EU is never going to trouble Uncle Sam on the Charlton Heston international index of shock and awe.

Despite Barack Obama's campaign aim of reducing military spending, he has increased it since he took office. He wants to add 65,000 troops to the Army and recruit 27,000 more Marines. The realities of dealing with wars on two fronts and

37   SIPRI Figures on 2007 Worldwide Defence Spending.

confronting the threat of al-Qaeda everywhere has put paid to such reductions for the foreseeable future, with 17,000 extra troops already deployed in Afghanistan in February. So even with the least bellicose US President in decades, the EU is never going to trouble Uncle Sam on the Charlton Heston international index of shock and awe.

If we're in a race, we're not troubling the Ben Johnson of arms stockpiling who's sprinting ahead, muscled arms pumping the air, chugging steroids like Mickey Rourke and well, thumping the bejesus out of all comers on the track, on the sidelines and in the stands for good measure. On Obama's watch, the CIA has been forced to close down its secret prisons and discontinue the use of torture on terror suspects, so the US army and navy just may go out of their way to remind the world that they're still the scariest military force on the planet whether they have black ops at their disposal or not.

TL: Title V, Section 2 TEU

32 The Treaty can always be changed, but only by 'us'.

The Treaty sets out a four-track procedure for Treaty amendment. The Treaties can be amended in the ordinary way, or they can also be amended by simplified procedures. It provides that the Council, if acting unanimously, can move from voting by unanimity to qualified majority voting.

It is not a 'self-amending treaty' as Sinn Féin posits it. Fine Gael TD Lucinda Creighton states that "this Treaty sets down a very clear and transparent process, the convention process, first used in 2002 in drawing up what are the bones of this Treaty and I think that that was a very positive process involving civil society, involving representatives from NGOs and I would like to see that repeated in the future."[38]

> Does this sound like a self-amending Treaty to you? It sounds like a great big bloody load of work.

The Treaty states *'If the European Council, after consulting the European Parliament and the Commission, adopts by a simple majority a decision in favour of examining the proposed amendments, the President of the European Council shall convene a Convention composed of representatives of the national Parliaments, of the Heads of State or Government of the Member States, of the European Parliament and of the Commission.'*

---

38   TD Lucinda Creighton, National Forum on Europe, 90th Plenary session.

This convention adopts by consensus a recommendation to a conference of representatives from each of the Member States who decide on whether to adopt the amendment. Does this sound like a self-amending Treaty to you? It sounds like a great big bloody load of work. Just reading about it wears one out! OK, OK, the Council does have the option not to convene a Convention if they feel that the amendment isn't a major issue that requires all the head-scratching and chin-wagging. It's this 'no biggie' clause that the No Campaign have fastened onto as evidence of a conspiracy to deny the people power. Bollox. In such a case when the Council decide (in which we have a vote) not to have a convention, they still have to convene a conference with representatives from all Member States to decide on the amendment anyway.

All amendments made under the simplified procedures would still have to be ratified by each Member State in accordance with its constitutional procedures – i.e. no change in the requirement for a referendum in Ireland.

So self-amending Treaty? Eh, no.

TL: Article 48 TEU

33 It will piss off the British Conservative Party.

The post-war years brought a consensus between the major British parties that membership of Europe was an important part of the UK's recovery and a guarantor of ongoing wellbeing. Euroscepticism in Britain centred around the wish to retain the pound both as a God-Save-the-Queen-we-used-to-have-an-empire-you-know-toot-on-your-tatty-tarnished-bugle-of-nationhood and more importantly to maintain an independent monetary system. But in 2000, current shadow foreign secretary and former Conservative Party leader William Hague started an anti-EU campaign that put Britain's membership back on the agenda. The rise of the Independence Party (UKIP) which advocates a withdrawal further pushed it up the agenda. So politics as usual: people will say anything, even when it clearly damages their economy to create a position for themselves and get into power. The Conservatives are playing politics with the UK's economy and they continue to do so, even when they're a shoo-in for the next Government anyway.

Pro-European former Tory frontbencher David Curry told BBC Radio 4's World At One: "It is essential that the Conservative Party confronts UKIP and does not try to compete with UKIP for the Eurosceptic vote." After the defeat of Ireland's first referendum on Lisbon, David Cameron pressed Gordon Brown to declare the Treaty "dead." Nice play, David. You keep this up and the comparisons to Blair will move from youth, vigour and haircuts to ruthlessness, arrogance and megalomania.

John Monks, head of the European Trade Unions and gregarious Mancunian put it thus to *100 Reasons* "I don't know what they're dreaming of – some kind of 'Britain against Europe'. We're back to 1940, the Spanish Armada and Napoleon...we've all got our national nervous breakdown issues and ours is something about the 'Finest Hour' when we were alone and you know what - it's bloody lonely. 1940 must've been very lonely and it's a distortion of British politics, but it's influential."

Let them get their own history sticks, the thieving mites. Let them get t-shirts with Guy Fawkes as Che Guevara and leave the tricolour alone.

UKIP MEPs caused a stir in the European Parliament this year by unfurling three metre-long placards and donning green T-shirts emblazoned in orange with the slogan 'Respect the Irish Vote'. Led by their leader Nigel Farage, the stunt was quickly quashed by the speaker and vitriolic Irish MEPs who were bemused at the sight of British Conservatives championing Irish rights at the EU. Ex-Fine Gael MEP Avril Doyle had a spirited go at Unionist Jim Allister for siding with Sinn Féin on the issue. Fianna Fáil MEP Brian Crowley tackled Farage for hijacking the Irish flag and using it as a 'tablecloth to put their drinks upon'. Farage had previously attacked Crowley for his 'insolent' attack on the Czech President Klaus when he browbeat him with tales of Crowley's freedom-fighting father. "I am from Ireland and I am a member of a party in government. All his life my father fought against the British domination. Many of my relatives lost their lives."[39] It's fun, browbeating a browbeater. When, as in this case, foreigners, literally or figuratively, wrap themselves in the tricolour and suddenly champion our rights, it does excite some entertaining puffing out of chests and mythologising of history. But that's

---

39   European Parliament transcripts, 5 December 2008

what it's for, right? Use your history as a stick to smack your enemies with and attack from on high, especially if they ever try to take up your history stick for their shadowy motives. Let them get their own history sticks, the thieving mites. Let them get t-shirts with Guy Fawkes as Che Guevara and leave the tri-colour alone.

In terms of other hysterical fringe elements, it's also disturbing that the British National Party (BNP) has won its first 2 seats in the European Parliament elections. But that's democracy for you – if the British people wish to punish the Labour government by voting to send representatives of a fascist anti-EU party to Europe, then so be it. Even David Cameron was sickened by the result and said "It brings shame on us that these fascist, racist thugs have been elected to the European Parliament." It brings shame on the Conservatives to share an anti-EU agenda with the BNP and it'll annoy both the 'fascist, racist thugs' and the Conservatives if Ireland votes Yes.

The European Parliament voted to ratify the Lisbon Treaty on 20 February 2008 with the result of 525 in favour, 115 against and 29 abstentions. So if as expected, the Conservatives sweep back into power with Labour taking the hit of public distress at their handling of the depression (let's call it what it is) and Cameron presses on with his policy of taking the UK out of Europe, we could find ourselves back in the situation of looking to Britain as a main export market. Now that would be fun, wouldn't it? In 2000 it was all about Cannes, Munich and Stockholm. In 2010 it could be Birmingham, Staines and if we're really lucky, Swansea. Can't wait.

TL: nowhere

34 It'll piss off Sinn Féin.

It is slightly problematic being told by ex-MEP Mary Lou McDonald that her party is pro-European Union: "Ireland's place is in Europe, at the heart of Europe, we are in good standing and we will remain so."[40]

Good standing? How long do they think we'll remain in good standing? So Sinn Féin (translated as 'Ourselves Alone') believe Ireland should be 'at the heart of Europe' despite the fact that the party have never once supported any of the European Treaties. Not once. So let us understand this correctly: they believe in the European Union, just not in any of the laws that underpin its existence and allow it to function. Right. Hmmm.

"I reject the badge of a bad European. I reject the badge of a Eurosceptic."[41] Reject away, Mary Lou, it's what you're good at. Unsuccessful SF MEP candidate Tomás Sharkey isn't a bad European: "I want to be the Irish-speaking MEP. We need more translators working in the European parliament... we could train translators and create more jobs on the European scene. I want to get Ireland back to work." Tomás is going to kickstart job creation by speaking Irish in Strasbourg. Genius idea.

In addition to claiming that Article 48 in Lisbon would lead to majority voting on taxation (untrue), they argue that the only thing that would protect the Irish people from entering an EU-wide consolidated tax policy would be the Irish Government of the day. Wait a second, isn't this a party of democrats telling us that we can't trust democracy? (As if we didn't know that!) But really, if you argue that we can't trust our directly elected Gov-

---

40   MEP Mary Lou McDonald, 90th session NFE, 3 April 2008
41   MEP Mary Lou McDonald, 86th session NFE, 31 Jan 2008

ernment to negotiate on our behalf with regard to EU policy, what do you want? I know, let's have a referendum on every EU proposal and list books like this can be written until the end of time. The only other way we'd be safe from ourselves apparently is if Gerry Adams is elected Taoiseach and the day that happens, half the country would move to Canada.

Wait a second, isn't this a party of democrats telling us that we can't trust democracy?

In the 2008 campaign, Sinn Féin complained that we would lose influence in Europe if we lost a Commissioner. So we can tick that off as sorted, unless of course, we vote No, continue under Nice and are thus compelled to reduce our Commissioner numbers. They said that Lisbon would lead to tax harmonisation and this issue has been laid to rest by our legal guarantees. Bizarrely enough, neutrality was the next big plank of their campaign. It sticks in the craw not a little to hear Sinn Féin lecturing the Irish people on the sacrosanct status of Irish neutrality and the dangers of increased EU militarisation. Well you could argue that theirs is an expert opinion on the dangers of armed conflict, if little else. (Neutrality: see Reason # 7, 8, 9) This issue has been put to bed. So what's left?

They cling to the stated view that a second No from Ireland would force the EU back to the negotiating table resulting in a better deal for Ireland. It won't. The EU will move on, deciding that it's more important to respect the twenty-three Member States who ratified Lisbon, rather than the last few who delay signing the Treaty, until Ireland votes.[42]

Mary Lou now says "It is deeply disappointing that the govern-

---

42   The Czechs, Germans and Poles are pending – see Reason #61.

ment does not intend to provide legally binding guarantees in the areas of workers rights and public services." The Protocol on Services Of General Interests guarantees States' ability to fund and run public services as they see fit. As for workers' rights, the attentive reader will find these championed throughout this book. See Reasons #14, 29, 45, 49, 72, 75 & 97.

So that's going to be the way it is: scare people into thinking that primary schools are to be bought by Pepsi and complain about the Charter of Fundamental Rights not going far enough, despite the fact that it goes way too far for British and Polish employers. If that's all they've got left, it looks like Joe Higgins and PANA are the only reasonable, if misguided, voices left in the No Campaign.

TL: Article 48 TEU

35 If we're not in the heart of Europe, we can't influence European policy.

Catherine Day, Secretary General of the European Commission says "Ireland's image in the European Union has been tarnished by the No vote. I can see every day that it has reduced our ability to shape and influence events in the European Union."[43]

Despite the 2003 reforms, the Common Agicultural Policy (CAP) under which Irish farmers have greatly benefited will be under serious pressure to be reviewed entirely before the end of the Doha round of the WTO talks. We need to maintain our position of influence in this debate. The banking crisis has already devastated Ireland's reputation abroad and we're back to being viewed as a banana republic whose embrace of the rules of international governance was cosmetic at best.

"Without being a member in good standing, and let me under-line those words, in good standing of the EU, how often would our Taoiseach have bilateral meetings with the Chancellor of Germany or the President of France? How would our opinions count at the Councils of Europe? Not at all would be a fair and accurate description."[44]

This is one of the the most pressing arguments for voting Yes. Ireland has always been able to wield more influence on the direction of EU policy than we should have had by dint of pop-ulation size or economic clout. As usual our people have been our strongest export – in this case many savvy Irish politicians and eurocrats.

---

43   Sub-Ctte on Ireland's Future in the European Union, Report Nov. 2008
44   Peter Sutherland, NFE, 3 April 2008

Of the five Secretaries-General of the European Commission since 1957, two (the current office-holder, Catherine Day, and her predecessor David O'Sullivan) were Irish. Currently, three Directors-General at the Commission and three of twenty-seven Commission Chefs de Cabinet are Irish.

> As usual our people have been our strongest export — in this case many savvy Irish politicians and eurocrats.

Former Fine Gael leader John Bruton, the Commission ambassador to the US, warns us that no Irish person was asked to sit on the Committee that was set up to examine the future of Europe post-Lisbon. The names of various prominent Irish figures had been bandied about prior to the naming of the Committee, but in the end none were chosen. Subsequently a committee was convened to investigate the pressing issue of cross-border banking supervision. Again no Irish person was selected to be on that committee. It is by being asked to participate on these committees that advise the Commission on shaping policy that Ireland can influence it and inclusion at this coalface relies on goodwill. Goodwill that we are perilously close to squandering entirely if we reject Lisbon after our amendments have been procured and guaranteed.

"Many ingredients have contributed to our success but none have been more important than goodwill. The goodwill of partners and EU institutions has been built up painstakingly through constructive engagement, several successful Irish Presidencies and respecting the concerns and aspirations of others." – Ambassador Bobby McDonagh, Permanent Representative of Ireland to the European Union.[45]

---

45   Sub-Ctte on Ireland's Future in the European Union, Report Nov. 2008

For years, savvy Irish politicians and Eurocrats have used all their diplomatic skills to broker deals between other Member States, while securing access to promote Irish interests. Access and influence are not established in black and white by law, but in person by contact and everyday dealings and things can change pretty quickly in Brussels.

TL: the lot in its entirety.

36 Ireland retains sovereignty of its legal system.

The central principle of Mutual Recognition ensures that individual legal systems of Member States are respected.

100 Reasons wishes to stress that this is not anything to do with the situation that occurs when you are winding down the street at a pace that cannot be sold to anyone as either swift, or even businesslike and you spot a terrifyingly familiar face floating towards you from twenty yards off and it clocks you at the same moment. Knowledge of prior encounters, encyclopaedic recall of its past jobs, partners and funny anecdotes all present themselves on time, but nary a whispered whiff of a name can besummoned forth.

Rictus-smile and an 'Alright Chief/Boss/Our fella' or cast your eyes to the pavement and barrel on.

Rictus-smile and an 'Alright Chief/Boss/Our fella' or cast your eyes to the pavement and barrel on. Nor is it that doffing of your proverbial hat and sheepish grin when you see another whipped-boyfriend/husband/father renting *Mamma Mia* with his lady. It's a different order of Mutual Recognition altogether.

This is a new innovation instead of harmonisation where standards across the EU are made fully consistent by imposing a common EU law.

Article 67 states *the Union shall constitute an area of free-*

dom, security and justice with respect for fundamental rights and the different legal systems and traditions of the Member States' and goes on to say *'the Union shall facilitate access to justice, in particular through the principle of mutual recognition of judicial and extrajudicial decisions in civil matters.*

It does not just pertain to civil matters, but also sets out the *mutual recognition of judgements in criminal matters and, if necessary, through the approximation of criminal laws.*

This makes the work of Eurojust and Europol much easier when combating cross-border crime of people and drugs trafficking.

TL: Articles 65 [81], 69A [82], 69D [85] TFEU

37 The Treaty keeps the Union 'co-operative'.

The Treaty junks the state-like elements of the Constitutional Treaty. The use of the terms 'Constitution', 'European Foreign Affairs Minister', 'laws' and 'framework laws' are dropped. The anthem and the motto are also dumped.

What was the motto? Maybe we could make one up instead... MOTTO: 'We as Europeans, like to stand tall inside the tent, shoulder-to-shoulder, buttocks clenched and chins thrust upwards and piss out the slit, instead of squatting slack-jawed outside, peeing in!'

OK, it's a steal from Lyndon Johnson, it doesn't rhyme and it would sound a lot, lot better in, like, Latin, but it gets a dig in at the UK for not joining the Eurozone.

We still have the flag, otherwise what will we lower to half-mast when Sophia Loren dies? And as for the anthem, what happened to that nice Beethoven hymn? You see, here's where it all went wrong for the Constitutional Treaty (well, apart from the decision to call it the 'Constitutional Treaty' with an, em, 'Constitution'.) We proud Europeans, but prouder Nationalists, got a whiff of bombast, a thick gust of ceremonial must clogged up our sinuses and through our watering eyes, we envisaged having to hum another (albeit, musically superior) tune at the start of football matches on top of our poxy atonal national anthems, so of course, we bucked and revolted.

It is amusing that it is one of the dumbest and bloodthirsty ideologies ever, i.e. nationalism, that has once again reared its ugly head to run off any perceived encroaching of European federalism. It really has done Europe wonders: two world wars, the Holocaust, Serbian ethnic cleansing, French nuclear testing, the Troubles. Them and us, them and us. Co-operate with other countries for mutual economic and cultural advancement? To hell with that. But once we see the chance of economic stability and of course, eh, continued peace in our time, we can't help gently stroking the European self-destruct button. It's just too easy, there's gotta be a catch.

But they shouldn't have given us the excuse, right? An anthem? I mean, really.

TL: throughout with a red line struck through them.

38 Helps Europe maintain coherent, positive relationships with its neighbours

The European Neighbourhood Policy will be given legal force. The ENP is being extended to include the EuroMed countries of North Africa and the Middle East, Eastern European countries like Moldova, Ukraine and Belarus, and certain Caucasian countries.[46]

The Union shall develop a special relationship with neighbouring countries, aiming to establish an area of prosperity and good neighbourliness, founded on the values of the Union and characterised by close and peaceful relations based on co-operation.

The 2008 Budget for this policy was €1.6 billion, so it's clearly taken seriously that close neighbours, especially those sharing territorial borders, are advantaged by their association with the EU and in time become viable trading partners.

Dick Roche told 100 Reasons "One of the things that they'll (the Neighbourhood policies) do is they will answer this continuous question about where does Europe start and where does it end." This was also a reference to Silvio Berlusconi's mischievous suggestion that if Turkey is allowed into the EU, then we should extend the invitation to Israel. The cheeky monkey. Roche goes on to say "It was very interesting to talk, particularly, to the North African countries about their take – because their take that this was an end to colonialism. Completely different view than people in Ireland sometimes have of it."

---

46   The Joke is, there is no joke, one can't be flippant about Moldova.

It's kind of like the big fella from up the road giving you a perfectly serviceable 2-year-old flatscreen, after he's gone and splurged in Harvey Norman for a new 90" plasma. Sure it's charity, but you're glad the big fella has taken an interest in you and you stand on the doorstep shooting the breeze afraid to let him in case he sees the stack of tabloids, ganja leaves and pizza boxes littering your living room floor. You lie and say you've a number of interesting projects on the boil, your fingers in many pies, a myriad number of investment portfolios. You decide from that day forth to clean up your act, to start buying the *Irish Times* instead of the *Sun*, *OK*, maybe start with the Indo, let's not be too hasty and resolve to sign off the scratcher (soonish, definitely within the next three months). As you thank him and close the door, you grumble that he could've wiped the film of dust off the screen, but maybe he's sending you a message. That he'll give you tellies, but you've still got to wipe the dust off on your own, yeah, maybe he's subtly offering you a job, yeah, he's recognised that the two of you are cut from the same cloth, aggressive alpha-male self-starters. Yeah, you'll definitely be able to wangle a job out of him – he likes you, you've got potential. To hell with it, you're a young country, you've still got a shot! You connect up your new TV, wipe it with some wet kichen roll and see your gaunt, unshaven face staring back at you. You grin and resolve also to get your teeth fixed – they're fairly manky.

It's just like that.

TL: Article 7A [8] TEU

39 Ireland's existing 'opt out/opt-in' protocol is preserved.

This relates to the area of criminal law and police co-operation in Title V of the Treaty on the Functioning of the EU. During the Treaty negotiations, Britain decided to exercise an opt-out in the area. This had ramifications for Ireland as we share common law systems, which are different from European legal systems. Ireland would have had to act alone in shaping proposals that would take account of our legal system and not leave us isolated in the EU.

The Sub-Committee on Ireland's Future in the European Union expressed concerns in the post-referendum report over Ireland adopting too many opt-outs from EU policy areas. It pointed to the Danish experience and the growing consensus that its opt-outs in the areas of Justice and Home affairs, the European Security and Defence Policy, and the Euro have had a detrimental effect on Denmark's national interests. In opting out of a specific area, the State loses its veto in any future votes in that area – this curtails its ability to influence the direction of European policy.

That's like saying saying your flatmate self-harms and her feet stink, but 'not in a bad way.'

Svend Auken, Chairman of the European Affairs Committee of the Danish Parliament states "I believe they [other Member States] look on this position [Danish opt outs] as self-deprivation and as a problem we have taken upon ourselves... Everybody looks on us as being weird or as the odd man out, but not in a negative way."[47] But 'not in a negative way'. That's like saying saying your flatmate self-harms and her feet stink, but 'not in a bad way.'

Our own opt-out allows Ireland to opt into future policies on a case-by-case basis. Ireland declared its intention to review the operation of the opt-out/opt-in device in 2012. Articulating the Labour perspective, Michael D. Higgins told us he believes "that the opt out/opt-in protocol provides us with useful flexibility to participate where we can and want to, and choose not to where we cannot or do not wish to. Ireland is not the same as Britain; Ireland is not the same as the rest of the EU; Ireland must chart its own course working in partnership and with respect for our fellow Member States."

If we wish to take part in a piece of mooted legislation that comes under our opt-out of Title V, we have three months after a proposal has been presented to the Council to notify the Council President in writing that we want in.

TL: Title V TFEU; Protocol on the Position of the United Kingdom and Ireland in respect of the area of Freedom, Security and Justice.

---

47 The Sub-Committee on Ireland's Future in the European Union, Nov. 2008 pg. 41

40 It encourages a wider gene pool.

It promotes the chance of Ireland achieving a viable gene pool by interbreeding with gorgeous people from the rest of Europe.

Voting Yes for Lisbon will encourage more sexy Europeans to our shores, who will eventually run out of men and ladyfolk of their own kind and be finally won over by our Oirish charm.

In short, it's the only act of patriotism left: if we want our sons and daughters to have green eyes, cheekbones you could skin a cat with, long legs and a musculature that's fit and svelte with bizarrely little need for exercise, then

> Let's face it, there's no Member State in the EU with a more bet-down population than ourselves...

we have to do everything in our power to encourage more Eastern Europeans to dull, grey Irish towns. The only thing to do in these places, during a recession, when it rains, on a Sunday is to engage in copious amounts of Irish-Latvian, Irish-Polish, Irish-Lithuanian, Irish-Hungarian, Irish-Czech Republican sexual activity leading to planned, unplanned, phantom and glorious new Euro-pregnancies. This next generation of super-Irish will be able to temper their goo for the sauce and wow folk with charisma *and* good looks – and that's never happened to us before.

Let's face it, there's no Member State in the EU with a more bet-down population than ourselves, (Estonia has got to be better-looking, I'm sorry) so let's not be fussy – old Europe is still damn good-looking. French people still won't sleep with us, no matter how much we wax on about Beckett, but Germans and Swedes are up for it as part of a rites of passage, social experiment list-type thing. Things to do before I marry at 31: military service, go Eurorailing, sleep with an Irish person. We won't form an uber-race out of these one-night-only charity/ experiential encounters, so it's best to keep learning Polish. They're pretty, they're feisty and they'll drink you under the table. Na zdrowie!

TL: Polish translation of the Treaty.

41 If it wasn't for Europe, Ireland would be bankrupt.

Being a member of the Eurozone and thus having a strong currency has been a great guarantee of the financial system and otherwise we would have gone bankrupt in the first few months of 2009.

Daniel Cohn-Bendit, the French/German firebrand of the Paris barricades in May '68 is these days a Green MEP (and still fond of spitting fire at his opponents). On the question of Ireland in Europe, Danny le Rouge said "Well today, the Irish know. They know how much they depend on the European Central Bank; that their policy of low corporate tax didn't save them; that the only thing saving them from the mess they're in is European protection. That's why they'll say Yes, because they have a strong sense of their national interest."[48]

Cohn-Bendit is a legend in European politics for telling it like it is and it was his spirited attack on Czech President Vaclav Klaus in December 2008 that so over-excited Fianna Fáil MEP Brian Crowley. He rattled the President so much that Klaus accused him of being the rudest man he'd encountered publicly in 19 years. If you don't like what people are saying to you, it's a neat way of dismissing them. Even after the Czech parliament passed Lisbon, Klaus insists on waiting on the second Irish referendum to ratify the Treaty.

Our own floppy-haired TV economist David McWilliams puts it thus: "Ironically, it looks as if the Irish banks – and also, by virtue of these unusual circumstances, the Irish government

48   Daniel Cohn-Bendit, *The Irish Times*, 17 April 2009

– have just found an all-forgiving priest in the guise of the European Central Bank. The ECB is keeping us afloat."[49] The Irish banking system has increased its dependence on the ECB for short-term finance from €30 billion before the liquidity crisis to a massive €130 billion now. But an important caveat to make is that it is not just the Irish banks that have racked up this total, it includes IFSC companies and there's a lot of them. Simon Carswell, the *Irish Times* money man told us "In the current financial climate, the benefit of being in the European Union is that the European Central Bank is providing life support for the Irish banking system and without it, it would be flatlining."

> It's a good job he already has a proper degree, as those honorary degrees aren't worth a curse. Sure even Bertie Ahern got one and he got us into this mess.

Citing the euro zone and the European Central Bank, the current High Rep Javier Solana says: "All these things contribute to make the crisis less difficult. Everybody would be in a much more difficult position without these institutions."[50] Now granted someone somewhere in some Brussels backstreet would probably slip old Javier some surreptitious yo-yos to say something like that, but all the same he would seem to have some weight of opinion behind him. In April, Javier donned the mortarboard in Belfield to have a honorary law degree conferred on him by UCD. It's a good job he already has a proper degree, as those honorary degrees aren't worth a curse. Sure even Bertie Ahern got one and he got us into this mess.

49   *The Sunday Business Post*, 24 May 2009
50   Javier Solana, *The Irish Times*, 23 April 2009

In February 2007, Economic and Monetary Affairs Commissioner Joaquin Almunia visited Ireland and warned us of the challenges of maintaining economic competitiveness and the dangers of globalisation. He cited European integration and Ireland's place in the Eurozone as beneficial to inflation figures, interest rates and its ability to attract foreign direct investment and our capacity to survive external shocks (ahem, we may laugh, but without the EU cushion effect, how would we fare?) He also cited migration flows from Poland and the Baltic States to here as highly helpful to employment levels and the economy. He said "Evolution in the Irish economy regarding competiveness since 1999 since the launching of the Economic and Monetary Union has not been seemingly a very positive one. Ircland has been losing competitiveness year after year."[51]

Now as of May 3rd 2009, he's predicting that the economy will shrink by 9 per cent this year rather than the 7.7 per cent than Minister for Finance Brian Lenihan predicted in the Budget. These Spaniards have got our back, but unfortunately they're pesky realists.

TL: It's not many Banks that continue to spew out cash, once 'insufficient funds' flashes.

---

51   ec.europa.eu, 8 February 2007

42 Lisbon strengthens Irish independence from Britain.

Without the EU, we are just a piss-poor region of the UK.

It's hilarious really. We expended all that energy for all those years shouting from the rooftops that whatever we were, we weren't British, we didn't want to rely on the UK and we were an independent nation state. By rejecting Lisbon we place ourselves back into a European club of two, us and a Conservative Party-led Britain. Genius move on our part. The Famine, Home rule, Easter Rising, civil war, free state, the Troubles. All seems like a huge amount of effort, suffering and carnage to achieve independence of identity, nationhood and to back it all up, economic freedom.

When we joined the EEC in 1973, 54 per cent of our exports went to the United Kingdom, with only 21 per cent going to the rest of Europe. Before we joined the European Monetary Union, the punt was tied one-to-one with sterling, meaning all monetary policy decisions occurred in the City of London. Only 18 per cent of our exports now go to the UK, compared with 45 per cent to the expanded European Union. It freed us from 130 years of total dependence on a British food market that pursued a 'cheap foods policy' against our small farms since 1846.

How do you forge a separate identity when you've got a strong neighbour? Well you cosy up to the even bigger boys like Uncle Sam and EU Sugar Daddy and play one off the other. It's a game we've been very good at, but while the economic dependence on Britain has apparently lessened, one look at the shopfronts or the TV schedules and you have to wonder. British cultural and economic colonialism has long since taken over the island. For about an eyeblink in the mid-90s, people seemed nonplussed by Dublin's Henry and Grafton streets suddenly being indistinguishable from any other British high street be it in Chester, Liverpool or Barnsley and then they just went with it. We were already familiar with all the UK chains from shopping trips to Newry, Sprucefield and post-bombscare Belfast. But Next, Boots, Dixons, PC World, A-Wear, Barretts, Burton, FCUK, HMV, Topshop, Warehouse, Principles, Argos, Dorothy Perkins, Jack Jones, Millets, Miss Selfridge, Monsoon, Mothercare, Mango, River Island, B&Q, Atlantic Homecare, Woodies DIY, Tie Rack, Harvey Nichols, Karen Millen, Marks & Spencer wanted in and we didn't have enough of our own fuck-off flagship name-brand stores to stem the tide, so we buckled and folded. Now a lot of this homogenisation comes precisely from being part of an internal market, but we shouldn't kid ourselves. The colonialism is complete.

> By rejecting Lisbon we place ourselves back into a European club of two, us and a Conservative Party-led Britain.

If you support a Premiership team, watch Sky News, go to Dundrum, Blanchardstown or any one of the identikit retail parks or 'villages' around the country buying your groceries in Tesco and clothes at the chains, read the *Sunday Times* and watch *Eastenders*, you're British by consumption, if not in accent or geography. You're also American when you shop at the Gap, watch anything at the multiplex and drink watery Budweiser in your local sports bar.

The process is so complete, it doesn't even have to be insidious anymore. It's overt – it's advertised. There are reactions to it of course. The brilliant programming of TG4 and resurgence of the GAA championing old sports with new mass appeal. The exporting of waves of Irish stand-up comedians to take over their sitcoms and panel shows and slag off British people while they do it. But there won't be a companion book *100 Irish Reactions to Cultural Colonialism* – we can think of two.

There's little doubt that Ireland's membership of the EU and participation in the Single European Market has been the most significant factor in ending our country's economic dependence on the United Kingdom and if we resume a closer economic relationship at the expense of international trade, our sovereignty is only so much stick-on waterproof tattoo.

TL: But you know, we speak the language so much better than they do...

43 Lisbon simplifies agricultural and fisheries Policy.

The Common Agricultural Policy (CAP) is extended to include fisheries under its voluminous cloaks. So the Common Fisheries Policy (CFP) is being merged into and swallowed with a burp by the Moby Dick of EU policy, the CAP. Henceforth, the term 'agricultural', shall be understood as also referring to fisheries. So the next time you go down to your uncle's farm, *100 Reasons* will be expecting some smoked mackerel to be slung over your shoulder upon your return (but only if you're wearing the wax, Squire-of-the-Market Barbour-type jacket, otherwise just carry them in a plastic bag, or maybe even double-bag it, to be on the safe side).

The aims of the CAP - securing food supplies, expanding output, increasing productivity, stabilising prices and securing incomes have been subject in recent years to an urgent need for reforms - reducing subsidies, reducing quotas – thus now cutting output, encouraging diversification and rewarding environmentally efficient farming methods. The aims of the CFP of maintaining marine ecosystems, protecting fish stocks, protecting the stakeholders in the industry and making such an industry sustainable are beset with the challenges of overfishing leading to dwindling stocks, difficulty in assigning quotas, a lack of property rights and what to do with damaged fishing communities.

Maritime Commissioner Joe Borg is serious about how much the CFP needs to be overhauled. "We are not looking for just another reform. We are asking questions even on the fundamentals of the current policy and should leave no stone unturned." The policy was last reviewed in 2002 and normally wouldn't be on the table again until 2012. But the situation has become too dangerous to wait. 88 per cent of European fish stocks are over-fished, compared with only 25 per cent worldwide. Almost one in three fish can't reproduce because th e parent population is so depleted. In the North Sea, 90 per cent of cod are caught before they spawn. Europe now imports two-thirds of its fish. There is still employment in fishing, but mainly in processing and pack-ing, as only 190,000 people are involved in the actual business of catching fish. However this is apparently still too many. The European fleet, even after repeated downsizing, of 88,000 ves-sels, is still too many boats chasing too few fish.[52] The quotas set by the EU on catches have so far failed to give the seas the time to re-stock and they are unpopular with fishermen, despite the subsidies given in recompense. A radical reform of the CFP is needed to make the European fishing industries viable again. A sea change is needed, as the CFP is not the leviathan from the deep threatening fishing jobs, it is fishing itself.

After IFA chief Padraig Walshe received reassurances from Brian Cowen before Lisbon I over WTO reform, he stated that his organisation would support the Treaty: "The way is now clear for farm families to vote Yes in the Lisbon Treaty Referendum."[53] This time they needed no extra prompting "We will visibly be supporting the Yes vote because we have more to lose than any other sector if we don't get a Yes vote on Lisbon." He appealed to farmers to separate the issues of savage cutbacks coming from Government and the advantage to farmers' incomes of Lisbon going through and said "I think there is more of a realisation around what Europe does really mean. What interest rates would we have currently if we were not part of Europe?"[54]

TL: Article 32 [38] TFEU

---

52   ec.europa.eu, Fisheries, 23 April 2009
53   RTE website, Lisbon Treaty section
54   *The Irish Times*, 22 July 2009

44 The Commission President would be elected in a more democratic way.

The Commission President would be elected jointly by both the representatives of the Member States in the Council and by the European Parliament. S/he will be chosen from one of the Commissioners nominated by the Member States. The Commission President is also a member of the Council to ensure proper communication between the bodies.

> The Commission remains the most powerful institution of the EU, but a lot of the clout of this executive branch of the Union has been devolved...

The Commission remains the most powerful institution of the EU, but a lot of the clout of this executive branch of the Union has been devolved (Reason #22) towards an increase in co-decision between the Council, the European Parliament and the Council of Ministers.

The Council acting by qualified majority proposes a candidate for Commission President to the European Parliament, while taking into account the Parliament elections. This candidate is elected by the Parliament by a majority of its component members. If the useless sod is a sub-Barrosoan specimen who finds that not enough MEPs actually like him (or her) enough to actually slap it out and elect, then the Council has to propose another ambitious multi-lingual, sharp-suited show-off within a month to the Parliament, who vote to endorse or not as the case may be. And if that doesn't work, well, we should all just give up on this whole idea of European consensus politics and go back to tribes, racial stereotyping, uniforms and a soupçon of synchronised fascist marching, just for the craic.

The innovation of having a longer-serving, elected Council President (Reason #1), untied to a national administration, will also wrest some power away from the Commission.

TL: Article 9D [17] TEU

45 Stronger social protection

A new 'social clause' greatly strengthens social protection.

Article 9 is the new 'social clause' whereby the social issues maintaining workers' rights and the aim towards full employment must underpin all EU policies.

In defining and implementing its policies and activities, the Union shall take into account requirements linked to the promotion of a high level of employment, the guarantee of adequate social protection, the fight against social exclusion, and a high level of education, training and protection of human health.

TD Joe Costello, the Labour spokesperson on Europe and Human Rights, stated "This Treaty has more in it in relation to workers' rights than any of the other Treaties. We have the Charter of Fundamental rights and we have the Social Clause which will mean that all new European Union legislation will actually be socially and equality proofed."[55]

> Article 9 is the new 'social clause' whereby the social issues maintaining workers' rights and the aim towards full employment must underpin all EU policies.

His party leader Eamon Gilmore also believes that this is a significant innovation that will permeate the whole legislative business of the EU. The Treaty goes further and the aim of a high level of employment in this article is increased to the

---

55   95th Plenary session, NFE, 1 May 2008

stated aim of 'full employment' in Article 2 (TEU).

The social clause goes on to say:

In defining and implementing its policies and activities, the Union shall aim to combat discrimination based on sex, racial or ethnic origin, religion or belief, disability, age or sexual orientation.

This is good news for 82-year-old black Korean autistic wheelchair-bound Mormon hetero ladies. It's also good news for the rest of us.

TL: Article 5a [9] TFEU

46 Sensitive laws subject to unanimity

Decisions on especially sensitive areas are made in the Council by unanimity guaranteeing Ireland's option to veto.

Two such sensitive areas are family law and the possible creation of a European Public Prosecutor.

A requirement of unanimity remains when deciding issues related to family law and any creation of the the European Prosecutor's office and broadening of its powers whose drafted remit only extends to financial wrongdoing for now, not criminal law.

The Public Prosecutor would be based with Eurojust and would liaise with Europol, Eurospar and Eurobaby at the Airside Motor Park.

The European Council may, at the same time or subsequently, adopt a decision amending paragraph 1 in order to extend the powers of the European Public Prosecutor's Office to include serious crime having a cross-border dimension and amending accordingly paragraph 2 as regards the perpetrators of, and accomplices in, serious crimes affecting more than one Member State. The European Council shall act unanimously after obtaining the consent of the European Parliament and after consulting the Commission.

The Public Prosecutor would be based with Eurojust and would liaise with Europol, Eurospar and Eurobaby at the Airside Motor Park. Interpol wouldn't get a look in baby, because well, it doesn't apparently exist anymore. Which makes me sad and nostalgic for Inspector Clouseau (the Peter Sellers version).

Right now, a continent-wide prosecutor looking into financial misdealings could very well be a terrific idea and might speed up the reform of the banking sector and of course, its Wild West, Dublin's IFSC. A new sheriff without any links to Irish government or business could be just what we need. It'll be interesting to see if we allow its establishment or veto it. And if we shoot him down cold before he's even got to push open the half-doors of the Harbourmaster and spit a brown watery wad of baccy out of the side of his mouth into a silver spitoon with a PING, what nasty robber barons would we be protecting?

How a State decides to deal with sensitive moral or ethical issues and its family law is always closely bound up with its national identity and the EU has no formal competences in these areas. These competences work on the basis of subsidiarity and Member States respect each other's position when it comes to family law.

This is one of the highly generous 'two for the price of one' reasons.

TL: Article 69E [86] TFEU

47 God remains optional

There's no 'In God We Trust' rubbish in Lisbon, but instead the Treaty amends the preamble to the Treaty on European Union (TEU) to include for the first time a reference to the *cultural, religious and humanist inheritance of Europe, from which have developed the universal values of inviolable and inalienable rights of the human person, freedom, democracy, equality and the rule of law.*

This is a sop to both sides really – in very general terms, it recognises the faiths that have been pivotal in forming the identity of the European countries, but it refuses to actually name them. A nice compromise – indeed a deft bit of negotiation that shows the EU's canny ability to build consensus out of two very different viewpoints! This must make the Irish Humanist Society very happy. They came out with an ad campaign earlier this year with the slogan 'Unbelievable' giving out about the compulsory requirement to make declarations referring to Himself, before one fills various public offices. They wanted the reference to the Most Holy Trinity in the preamble to Bunreacht na hÉireann to be removed and various articles dealing with oaths and blasphemy excised. Oaths and blasphemy are fun, though – you can wind up an awful lot of people with a good oath and bit of blasphemy. It is difficult to understand what exercises them so much – if there's no God, what's the problem in swearing an oath to him? He doesn't mind – he can't, he doesn't exist.

To be absolutely fair to these people, they're not nutjobs, just nice folk with far too much time on their hands. Yes, perhaps we should get rid of it eventually, but a national poster campaign? Really? They may have been influenced by their British counterparts who, led by amongst others, inveterate shit-stirrer Richard Dawkins, had run a bus poster campaign with the slogan 'There is probably no God, so stop worrying and enjoy your life.' I think the British Humanists trumped them in the memorable catchphrase stakes.

The Government wanted a reference to the Big Man up(or not)stairs, but they were pleased that the Treaty at least explicitly states that the Union shall respect the status of churches and religious organisations under national law.[56] It also welcomed the provision for open, transparent and regular dialogue with churches and religious organisations, which is established by the Treaty.[57]

The Catholic Bishops of Ireland Pastoral reflection on Lisbon opened with "Unless the

> If there's no God, what's the problem in swearing an oath to him? He doesn't mind — he can't, he doesn't exist.

Lord builds the house, those who build it labour in vain" (Ps 127:1). So we can take it they're a bit miffed at the lack of a mention for the Lord our Saviour. They describe the omission as 'regrettable', but gain some succour from the fact that the aims of the EU are underpinned by Christian ethics about how a society should be organised. Roger Cole of PANA believes 'the devil's in the detail'. So it's best to keep both big guys out of the text, otherwise it would just give confirmed atheist Joe Higgins another excuse to grumble and we'd risk provoking Chris de Burgh into an uncalled for Indian summer of religious songwriting.[58]

TL: Preamble to TEU

---

56   Article 16C [17] TFEU
57   Government White Paper on the Lisbon Treaty 2009, DFA, July 2009, pg. 29
58   culminating in a new album *Portuguese Express*.

48 More democracy!

The Qualified Majority Voting procedure enacted with Lisbon is made even more democratic by dint of the Ioannina Compromise.

The 'Ioannina Compromise' is not the title of a Robert Ludlum book, a Len Deighton book, a Dan Brown book nor a EU Media-funded Europudding film starring Roger Moore, Telly Savalas and child star Matt Damon as 1980s be-mulleted Mediterranean pirate spy mercenary eco-fishermen. It's none of these things.

A decision to make peace with a tosspot brother-in-law, you might call 'The Dunboyne D'entente'

The Ioannina Compromise takes its name from an informal meeting of Foreign Affairs ministers in Ioannina in Greece in 1994. The question arose of the possibility of having a compromise in qualified majority voting in an enlarged (then) fifteen-Member community. If members of the Council representing between twenty-three votes (the old blocking minority threshold) and twenty-six votes (the new threshold) expressed their intention of opposing the taking of a decision by the Council by qualified majority, the Council would do all within its power, within a reasonable space of time, to reach a satisfactory solution that could be adopted by at least sixty-eight votes out of eighty-seven.

The compromise measure was made redundant by the Nice Treaty, but it came up again during the negotiations on Lisbon. Upon ratification, a new version of Ioannina would come into force from 2014.

It enables a group of states close to the minority blockage – but who have not achieved this – to request the re-examination of a decision adopted by the qualified majority in Council.

Why doesn't everyone start naming the diplomatic turning points of their lives after the towns in which they happened? You've just patched things up with an old schoolmate you haven't spoken to since he snogged your ex: you could call it 'The Rathangan Rapprochement'. A decision to make peace with a tosspot brother-in-law, you might call 'The Dunboyne D'entente' or perhaps these moments of momentous truce could relate to inner calming: 'The Enniscorthy Epiphany' or 'The Red Cow Realisation' (which should really be never to traverse this hellish junction ever, ever again, as it represents the nadir of Irish civilisation.) Placenames should however never be utilised by one's partner to commemorate worrying episodes of sexual underperformance: 'the Drumcondra Inadequacy' would be be just too, too cruel.

Perhaps exotic Mediterranean towns are needed to give even Irish personal/political alliances and power-shifts some heft, so it would seem fair that one could name the compromise after the sunny holiday one books in dizzying relief at another conflict averted – 'the Tenerife Termination'. (Oh apologies, that actually refers to the cause of more Irish relationship break-ups than infidelity, mental cruelty and the drink: package holidays.)

TL: working agreement by all Member States not present in Treaty.

49 Greater protection for workers

The Globalisation Adjustment Fund (GAF) is to be reformed and extended.

The €500 million fund was established in 2006 to help workers made redundant as a result of unexpected changes in world trade to access training and get back to work.

Amendments to the GAF will allow Member States apply for support when 500 workers are let go, rather than the 1000 requirement at present. The EU will also pay 65 per cent of the cost of retraining schemes, up from the 50 per cent currently offered.

"Crucially, the scheme has been extended to cover businesses that shed jobs due to the current crisis rather than just shifting patterns of world trade – a requirement that may have caused problems for an application covering job losses at Dell."[59]

This annual €500 million cushion against the vicissitudes of globalisation is never more needed than right now. The GAF supports people rather than companies or institutions through measures like counselling, providing mobility allowance, new ICT (Information & Communication Technology) skills or other training and entrepreneurial support, including microgrants. These measures are meant to fall under 'active' types of support to assist re-employment of the targeted workers, rather than passive forms of social protection like unemployment benefit. The GAF aims to fund 50 per cent of the cost of support with the remaining 50 per cent being the responsibility of the Member State.

---

59   Jamie Smyth, *The Irish Times*, 14 April 2009

The fund comes into play on the request of a Member State, when a multinational company announces mass redundancies due to a structural changes in world trade patterns. The fund only intervenes when the redundancies have a significant negative effect on one region or industry, thus when the hardship caused has an EU dimension.

Of course, even though Sinn Féin have never supported any EU Treaty, they are very quick off the mark in realising what EU funds make them look good to constituents. The party website proudly proclaims that Sinn Féin MLA Raymond McCartney tabled a question to UK Department of Trade and Enterprise Minister Nigel Dodds to ask if

> This annual €500 million cushion against the vicissitudes of globalisation is never more needed than right now.

he has applied to the GAF to access funding for workers laid off by Seagate in Limavady. He said "It is important that once the clamour over the loss of jobs dies down that the workers of Seagate are not forgotten and that we strive to get the best package available to allow these people to return to a working environment."[60] And *100 Reasons* couldn't agree more.

TL: not present, but its deployment is dependent on good standing in EU.

---

60   Sinn Féin website

50 Guarantees the European Central Bank its independence

The European Central Bank has true independence from any meddling by the Member States and the other EU institutions.

The European Central Bank shall have legal personality. It alone may authorise the issue of the euro. It shall be independent in the exercise of its powers and in the management of its finances. Union institutions, bodies, offices and agencies and the governments of the Member States shall respect that independence.

The ECB presides over the European System of Central Banks (ESCB). The system's primary goal is to maintain price stability, while not messing up the EU's other economic goals. The ECB conducts the monetary policy of the Eurosystem, controls foreign exchange operations, holds and manages the official foreign reserves of the Member States and promotes the smooth operation of payment systems.

> So the ECB pulls up a couple of chairs for them in the corner and tells them to shut up and listen.

So in the same way that the National Central Banks are independent of government and its institutions, the same holds at European level. The Council President and a member of the Commission are allowed to sit in on meetings of the ECB's Governing Council, but they are not granted a vote. So the ECB pulls up a couple of chairs for them in the corner and tells them to shut up and listen.

Then when the Council is discussing matters that relate to the work of the ESCB, the President of the ECB is invited to participate.

No Campaigner Susan George says "We have a completely independent central bank so that there is no parliamentary control or even Council or even Commission control over monetary policy."[61] Um, yes, you're kind of making our point for us there, Susan, thanks. Like all of the National Central Banks, it has independence from government pressure, but that does not mean that the Council or Commission have no influence over monetary policy and it is disingenuous to suggest an independent Central Bank is anything but proper.

TL: Article 245a [282] TFEU; Protocol on the Statute of the European System of Central Banks and of the European Central Bank

---

61   NFE, Plenary sessions, pg. 166

51 Provides political assistance for trouble spots

The EU was highly supportive of the peace process in Northern Ireland in setting up a task force to assist specifically in resolving this issue.

The EU's PEACE programmes played a key role in promoting peace and have granted more than €1.2 billion in EU funding to projects in Northern Ireland and border counties since 1994.

As the root causes of the Troubles were economic disparities between communities and inequality of access to opportunity for education and decent work, it is unsurprising that the economic advantages that the Common Market wrought on both sides of the border helped to consolidate the peace through building business links between loyalist and nationalist communities and between North and South (and of course between Northern Ireland and the rest of the EU).

Proud Dundalkman and Minister for Justice Dermot Ahern goes all misty-eyed and recalls "the way in which the Single European Act... had the dramatic effect in my area of doing away with all the cross-border checkpoints which had a very practical effect for my town and indeed for towns like Newry on the other side whereby there used to be five-mile queues of traffic waiting to cross the border – they all disappeared overnight because of the Single European Act which was in fact brought in by Qualified Majority Voting."[62]

The latest tranche of funding under the Peace III programme

---

62   Minister Dermot Ahern, *The Pat Kenny Show*, 6 June 2008

was €21 million announced on April 20th 2009. Applications to Peace III greatly exceeded the Fund's capacity to support, but forty-five projects supporting 140 jobs will be receiving grants. Jim Dennison, the director of the Community Relations Council European programme said "This proves that there is a very genuine and sustained commitment to improving community life and relations in Northern Ireland. This is particularly noteworthy given recent attempts to destabilise the political process."[63]

The reconciliation and peace-promotion initiatives receiving funding include the Transcending Trauma project, which is run by Armagh-based Restorative Action Following the Troubles (RAFT); and Whatever You Say, Say Something, which is coordinated by Healing Through Remembering and the Crosslinks project, which is run by the Belfast-based Youth Initiatives organisation. There is a further €29 million to be injected by Peace III into the CRC's projects in the coming years that will further improve cross-community relations.

It's worth noting that the politicians who requested the task force be introduced like Martin McGuinness and Ian Paisley saw no contradiction in voting against this and all EU Treaties. As the years go by, the Chuckle brothers just keep finding more and more things in common. It must be lovely for them.

TL: the EU has played a large part in promoting peace in the North, managing to overlook the gargantuan egos of politicians on both sides and their stubborn need to hang onto outmoded nationalist and loyalist agendas in order to justify their very existence. Goodnight sweethearts, it's time to retire.

---

63   *Belfast Telegraph*, 20 April 2009

52 We keep the Common Travel Area.

Ireland and the UK decided to opt-out of the Schengen agreement (implemented by the Amsterdam Treaty in 1997) that dropped border controls across the EU. Both states decided to continue with the Common Travel Area of minimal border controls between the two States, the Isle of Man, Jersey and Guernsey, because the UK wished to retain its right as an island nation to enforce strict immigration controls between itself and continental Europe.

The European impulse towards a freeing up of travel and lifting of border controls across Europe has slowed since 9/11 which has seen costly and cumbersome security checks hastily introduced to international airports. 'Gastarbeiter' are welcomed in the boom-times, but their motives are questioned if they decide to stay in less promising times.

Freedom of movement within the EU to pursue employment is one of the most important aims of the Union that makes sense on any level – in minimising racism, boosting the economy and encouraging a cultural mix. These aims to promote an ethical EU-wide immigration policy affecting both EU citizens and non-Member State nationals are always going to take a backseat in times of security crisis and economic doom.

In 1985, the Benelux countries, France and Germany, held a series of conferences in Schengen, which was fittingly enough a border town in Luxembourg. The series of multilateral agreements they negotiated on cross-border movement of peoples came into force in 1995 and quickly were extended to include other EU Member States.[64] The best-known measure was the gradual dropping of border checks. This common zone of travel for EU citizens meant in practice that international borders were now barely noticed as cues like changes in road markings and flags were the only things alerting them to crossing frontiers. Transport companies had lobbied hard for this lifting of checks. I'm sure a few ambitious criminals weren't devastated by the idea either. It certainly necessitated far closer co-operation and information-sharing between police forces in tracking cross-border crime.

Within Schengen there are agreements between neighbouring countries to allow reciprocal 'hot pursuit' of suspects 10km into each other's territory by one another's police forces. Now while there have been many successful cross-border joint Garda/PSNI operations against dissident republicans and illicit fuel smugglers, it is hard to see the day when PSNI officers would be coming to within the outskirts of Dundalk in 'hot pursuit' of slippery Southern criminals or Gardaí would be belting towards Derry with sirens wailing.

> It is hard to see the day when PSNI officers would be coming to within the outskirts of Dundalk in 'hot pursuit' of slippery Southern criminals...

The troublesome aspect of the Common Travel Area is that its freedoms only extend to British and Irish citizens, so it presents challenges to immigration officials on both sides of the border trying to tell the difference between EU citizens, illegal immigrants, asylum seekers, foreign tourists and cit-

---

64   *The implications for Ireland and the UK arising from the development of recent EU policy on migration.* Piaras Mac Éinrí, Irish Centre for Migration Studies, NUI Cork.

izens of the two States. This leads to messy, embarrassing and offensive situations of officials stalking up and down the Enterprise train asking anyone of a swarthy hue or possessing any demonstrably foreign-looking physical characteristics for identification. This unofficial policy is undoubtedly racist, based on dangerous assumptions and sadly understandable. Irish people with foreign parentage, British people from all over the world and indeed either with tans and beards are regularly asked for ID. Students have been known to feign foreign customs just to create an entertaining public conflict, as they whip out a crumpled pink driving licence to be waved with derision at officialdom. How are they supposed to recognise Manx people freely entitled to the provisions of the CTA – by the fact that they have no tails?

However, there is no point in Ireland adopting the full tenets of Schengen without Britain on board too, so we limp on with an imperfect system that allows the local economies of border areas to continue with minimal bureaucratic disruption, but one side or t'other has upset many legal visitors to the island over the years.

TL: Protocol integrating the Schengen acquis into the framework of the European Union

53 Cheaper mobile phone calls

The EU has intervened to lower mobile phone charges across a newly created single Telecoms market.

New rules on text messaging and data roaming were passed in the European Parliament in April and came into effect from July 1st. The cost of a text message sent in the EU has been capped at 11 cents while it was previously 28 cents. The cost of calls made while roaming in another EU country now capped at 43 cents will gradually fall to 35 cents per minute by July 2011, and from 19 to 11 cents for mobile calls received while roaming abroad. This was always the killer − whenever you go on holiday and work colleagues continue to call you about work issues *and* you end up getting charged for it − now that's annoying.

Due to a lucrative kink in the billing system, mobile users were overcharged by up to 24 per cent for calls and now operators will no longer be able to continue this rounding-up practice and be forced to actually bill by the seconds used. Taken all togther, EU mobile users are expected to see a 60 per cent saving on their bills for when they are roaming in the EU. That's not to be sniffed at.

Data roaming charges have also been tackled, with vast disparities in the costs in different EU countries. Web browsing roaming charges have been capped wholesale at €1 per megabyte. This will mean a lot to Irish consumers, as the average EU wholesale charge was €1.68, but the charge here weighed in at a whopping €6.82. Did you ever feel violated? By your phone? So thank you EU, those business trips and holidays will feel a lot safer without worrying about the bulging paper intruder winging its way to your hall carpet a month later.

"Today's vote marks the definite end of the roaming rip-off in Europe," said EU Telecoms Commissioner Viviane Reding. "Thanks to the strong support of the European Parliament and the Council, the new roaming rules were agreed in the record time of just seven months. Just in time for the summer holidays, European citizens will now be able to see the single market without borders on their phone bills."[65]

Did you ever feel violated? By your phone?

Not only that, but the Commission has persuaded the main companies to back Europe-wide charger harmonisation. No more frantic rifling through office drawers and muttering "No, a 'Hello Moto' Motorola is no bloody use to me!" as you pitch dusty black plastic into the bin. When a colleague triumphantly thrusts a same-brand plug at you, you've been quick to scold "Not the old fat Nokia! The new thin, needly Nokia, before my phone – it's just died, thanks a lot." From next year, all phones from the main players will be compatible with standard chargers.

Whatever about fixing the chargers issue, the rapacious operators are not particularly happy about their call rates dropping. On April 28th 2009, our own Big Two, Vodafone and O2 joined forces with Deutsche Telekom's T-Mobile unit and France Telecom's Orange to challenge the 2007 EU law instituting the cap on roaming charges at the European Court of Justice. A barrister for Vodafone, David Pannick, told the Luxembourg court that the EU imposed a blanket widespread regulation without first seeing whether there's a 'less intrusive' remedy.[66] What? Less intrusive to your client's outrageous profits? These prohibitive charges hampered EU citizens in conduct-

65   ec.europa.eu, April 2009
66   John Collins, *The Irish Times*, 29 April 2009

ing their business and personal communications while abroad in Europe, so the swollen fingers of compulsive text messagers are being crossed across the continent as we await the result of the battle between big business and EU regulators. Judging by the fact that the caps have already come into force, *100 Reasons* reckons the score is EU: 1, Mobile Operators: 0.

TL: I'm ringing Lisbon while 'roaming' in Northern Ireland to check.

54 We get to stay in the EU.

A second No vote could force Ireland to give up its membership of the EU entirely.

Mr. Graham Watson, leader of the European Liberal Democrats, stated that "it is very difficult to see any country being
able to stay in if they have had two Nos from the people," when
Fianna Fáil joined the MEP's party in the European Parliament in March.[67]

The Liberals are the third-biggest group in the European
Parliament, with 80 MEPs, while there are four Liberal EU
Member State prime ministers and seven commissioners.
Scare tactics? The dream status of Ireland as the only English-
speaking country in the Eurozone and all-round economic
powerhouse shoring up loads of Foreign Direct Investment
from US multinationals soured in an eyeblink. This writer
is scared he won't have a job when he gets to number 100,
so yes it's scare tactics borne out of a very real situation that
we've gotten ourselves into and will need assistance digging
ourselves out of.

The Czech ex-foreign minister Karel Schwarzenberg said he
also thought his parliament would ratify the treaty; that failure to do so would leave his country "absolutely isolated" in
central Europe.

"For us, that would be an awful result. Ireland as an island at
least has free access to the sea. We are fully surrounded by the
EU. We would thus isolate ourselves within it," he said.[68]

---

67   *The Irish Times*, 6 March 2009
68   *The Irish Times*, 30 March 2009

Free access to the sea, you say? Yup, that's what's gonna save us. When the economy sinks under the weight of its own hubris and the country is going the way of Atlantis, we're going to swim for it and hope that when we get to Ellis Island, they're even half as accommodating as fifty years ago.

If we were to leave the EU, we could pursue some special relationship with the EU (they send us a Christmas card every year and apart from that, we never get invited to any of their parties) or we could join the European Economic Area with Norway, Iceland and Liectenstein. Now Norway's doing OK, but Iceland is begging to be let into the EU proper and the only time Liectenstein comes up in relation to Ireland, it's about very friendly soccer friendlies (this is a team Malta demolished 7-1 in 2008) and tax havens. Let's keep it that way.

> When the economy sinks under the weight of its own hubris and the country is going the way of Atlantis, we're going to swim for it...

TL: the 'Get the Fuck!..' Protocol

55 Finally, that annoying and confusing difference between the E.C. and E.U. is resolved.

Phew – what a Euro-mare. The 'European Union' shall replace and succeed the 'European Community.'

So around the back of a tall, grey Brussels building (built circa 1973) the bloated, lifeless corpse of the EC lies prone in a blue skip with yellow stars on it. No state funeral, no fanfare, no flag draped over its corpse, just chucked out on the street, disposed of, decommissioned.

> Around the back of a tall, grey Brussels building, the bloated, lifeless corpse of the EC lies prone in a blue skip with yellow stars on it.

But perhaps you'd prefer to imagine the EC living out its years under an acronyn protection scheme in a Lisbon time-share under a new name, the CG (Common Gardeners), or even worse, the PD (Progressive Demo- wait a second, haven't we...?) Whatever you care to imagine, EC: no more, EU: come on down, your time is now!

The only 'EC' around these days is the European Commission. To steal the tagline from *Highlander:* There can only be one.

TL: Throughout

56 Greater economic opportunities

The operation of the Common/Single European/Internal-oh-whatever-it's-called-now Market will be improved.

"The single market is as important to us as the air we breathe. We export 80 per cent of everything we produce and need access to markets. Our being part of an EU second tier or an also-ran group of countries could not really be considered as a viable option." – Frank Ryan, Chief Executive Officer, Enterprise Ireland[69]

Being the only English-speaking Member State of the Euro-zone and having access to the single market – now called the internal market – has been of the utmost benefit to Ireland.

Ireland, with only 1 per cent of the EU's population, attracted 25 per cent of all new US investment in Europe in the decade up to 2005. Since the establishment of the Single European Market in 1993, foreign investment here increased by more than 400 per cent. When Ireland joined the EEC in 1973, our GDP per capita was 58 per cent of the European average, and 54 per cent of our exports went across the Irish Sea, with only 21 per cent going to the rest of Europe. By the end of 2007, Irish GDP per capita had reached 144 per cent of the EU average. Only 18 per cent of our exports now go to the UK, compared with 45 per cent which go to the expanded European Union. Multinational companies have considered access to European markets as a key factor in making their investment decisions.[70]

---

69   Sub-Ctte Report on Ireland's Future in the EU, Nov. 2008, pg. 29
70   Sub-Ctte Report on Ireland's Future in the EU, Nov. 2008, pg. 19/20

The Lisbon Treaty largely leaves provisions related to the movement of goods, persons, capital, services and state aids unchanged, but future decision-making in relation to the social security arrangements is necessary to allow for the free movement of workers is to be by QMV, instead of unanimity.

However, where a Member State considers that a proposed measure *would affect fundamental aspects of its social security system, including its scope, cost or financial structure* it may request that the matter be referred to the European Council, which operates by consensus. This is our 'emergency brake'.

TL: Article 2 [3] TEU; 42 [48] TFEU

57 More efficient information-sharing between member states

The Conference of Parliamentary Committees for European Affairs would be established.

The conference is established to increase co-operation and information exchange between the National Parliaments of the Member States and the European Parliament.

It will assist the Joint Committees on European Affairs to learn from their European counterparts in an institutionalised setting. The Joint Committees have already learnt a great deal from the Danish Parliamentary Committee in terms of how to be fully proactive in its dealings with the European Parliament and the Commission. The Danes are held up to be a standard bearer in the area of early 'upstream' consideration of possible EU legislation.

> The way we can monitor legislation proposed by the Commission is through our own Parliamentary committees.

Lisbon greatly increases the power of National Parliaments. The way we can monitor legislation proposed by the Commission is through our own Parliamentary committees. It can only then be advantageous to them to compare and contrast how other committees play the watchdog role, to see what resources in terms of staff and finance they have at their disposal and how they divide up the work. In addition, on contentious issues, it would be necessary to know how the elected representatives of other Member States are leaning with regard to specific legislation.

A conference of Parliamentary Committees for Union Affairs may submit any contribution it deems appropriate for the attention of the European Parliament, the Council and the Commission.

It would mean more trips to Brussels for our dedicated Euro gatekeepers to educate themselves more deeply about how the EU actually functions and forge links with influential insiders OR it could just present another opportunity for them to raid the mini-bar and charge the Irish taxpayer. The reality? A little of bit of both.

TL: Protocol on the role of National Parliaments in the European Union

58 St. Columbanus would want you to vote for Lisbon.

He was the sixth century Irish missionary who first acknowledged Europe as a continental reality – '*Totius Europae*'. He's a pretty good contender for the title of first European.

Columbanus was reputed to have been quite the dashing young man and he came to the difficult conclusion that the only way to avoid the attentions of the voluptuous, brazen hussies of his home village of Nobber, Co. Meath was to get himself forthwith, haste, post-haste to a monastery. His poor auld Momma did not think that this was a very good idea at all and lay across the threshold of the family home to stop him going. But he manfully subdued his feelings of familial love (and lust for the Nobber lovelies) and stepped over Momma dearest and made his escape. Many young Irish men still have the experience of their Mommas blocking the exits trying to keep them home an extra night to feed them up and keep an eye on them, so they too must take brave Columbanus' lead and flee their Mommas (but not so much the brazen hussies).

Columbanus spent many years in chaste solitude at Lough Erne and Bangor monasteries and was pretty good at keeping on the straight and narrow with fervent prayer and scholarly works. Around the age of 40, he started hearing a voice that sounded awful like the Dear Lord himself yabbering at him incessantly about preaching the Gospel to the heathens of Europe. So he somehow convinced his Abbot it wasn't a mid-monastic life crisis, that he wasn't schizophrenic or that the horniness for some Eurotrash hadn't finally gotten the better of his loins. The Abbot bought his story and off he sailed with 12 buddies to Cornwall. They quickly got bored hanging with the crusty Anglo-Saxons and set off soon after for Brittany. He presented himself to Gontrum, the King of Burgundy, who kept up on his religious celebrities and figured by the preceding reputation and the cut of the handsome devil before him that Columbanus was the real deal. The King set him up in some nice digs at the Roman fortress of Annagray. Columbanus and his boys lived simply, while nobles and peasants came to visit, drawn by his reputation as a holy dude.

Later the number of disciples flocking to him obliged the poor creature to establish another Abbey at Luxeuil and a third at Fontaines. He instituted a perma-choir, or a perpetual service of praise, by which choir succeeded choir day and night, which was an early precursor of both 24-hour Euro news

Around the age of 40, he started hearing a voice that sounded awful like the Dear Lord himself yabbering at him incessantly about preaching the Gospel to the heathens of Europe.

and MTV or, to keep it in the EU, Music Channel TVK Lumea (it's Romanian). It may have made an awful racket and confused the wildlife, but that's what he wanted – musical praising day and night. Spike Jonze would've loved it.

All was well until the local bishops started dark mutterings about him, this rockstar Irish Abbot who had plonked down in their midst. They objected to his grá for Celtic Easter and admonished him for it. He wrote off to il Papa, Pope St. Gregory, and felt that Satan had intervened when he got no response, when it was just that the Italian postal system was shite and the Pope had died in the time the last letter took to arrive. How very frustrating. The monarchy was now in the hands of King Thierry who was fond of a bit of debauchery of the concubinage form and Columbanus had to give him a good talking to. Thierry responded by having him arrested and Columbanus decided to it was time to make a hasty, yet saintly escape.

Columbanus believed in the free movement of migrants in search of work and he upped sticks. This was the period when he really embraced Europe visiting Nevers, Nantes, Soissons, Metz and Mainz. He travelled down the Rhine preaching the Gospel and got to Zurich. He kept facing persecution and kept having to move on. Eventually he crossed the Alps into Italy. Here he was granted a wee plot of land in Bobbio, between Milan and Genoa to set up his little shop of the Holies.

His journeys into Europe were held up as the blueprint for subsequent European missions. The lesson *100 Reasons* supposes that we're to take from Columbanus's travels is that it's always a good idea to broaden your horizions beyond Nobber, Co. Meath, Italy's a good spot for an apartment and never mind the jealousy of local holymen, if your own brand of the Gospel is stronger, it's a free market.

TL: Don't be daft

59 If Lisbon isn't ratified, we will revert to the Treaty of Nice.

Do the No Campaigners who rejected Nice realise that by rejecting Lisbon, we will revert to Nice?

It is legally possible for the Union's business to continue on the basis of the existing Treaties and the institutional arrangements they set out, but this is unlikely given the will amongst the other Member States for reform. There is pressure from the aspirant States on the EU's periphery to enlarge even further and the Union has already been significantly weakened by such swift bang expansion by twelve Members in the past five years and thus made unwieldy with twenty-seven Members. A two-tier Europe is more likely to evolve and we'll be on the lower tier.

> The idea that a No vote would allow us to go back to the table and negotiate a better deal for Ireland is naïve and put forward in a cynical way.

Members of the No Campaign like Sinn Féin have supported none of the EU Treaties, so it can't be a reversion to Nice that they want. The idea that a No vote would allow us to go back to the table and negotiate a better deal for Ireland is naïve and put forward in a cynical way. Alexander Stubb, Foreign Minister of Finland says "I would see [renegotiation] as a very difficult option... To go back and reopen the whole package would be a little unrealistic."

The likelihood is that business will continue more on an intergovernmental basis between the six large Member States, lessening the ability of smaller States like Ireland to influence EU policy. Catherine Day (who's Irish), the Secretary General of the European Commission, says this and it's worth quoting her whole remark.

"I think the other Member States are keen to accommodate Ireland in terms of providing reassurances, but I do not see any willingness to reopen the treaty or go through a process of re-ratification. It has not been easy in some Member States to get to the current stage. The prospect of opening up the treaty and changing it does not seem to me to be feasible at all. It is a question of Ireland working out what it wants to ask the other Member States. There is enormous goodwill to try to find accommodations for Ireland, but that goodwill does not extend to changing the treaty."[71]

Despite the fact that a firm legal guarantee was hammered out in December that agreed to amend Lisbon to retain one Commissioner per State, if the Treaty is rejected the Member States are legally obliged to reduce the number of Commissioners by November 2009, as the Nice Treaty sets out.

Funny that, huh?

TL: see Nice Treaty, a rollicking read

---

71 Both quotes: Sub-Ctte Report on Ireland's Future in the EU, Nov. '08, pg. 27

60 Carla Bruni wants us to.
And what Carla wants, Carla gets.

She's never been denied anything before and we're kind of scared by her voracious appetites. Besides if she turned her back on us, we'd miss the golden sunshine of her smile, the sharp glint of her incisors, the steely gaze, those iron thighs. She'd be so pissed off with us, she might stop her bewildering visits to the Jools Holland show, (the best music show not on Irish TV) where the steady flow of saliva cascading down Jools' chin threatened to slide him off his piano stool. She might force NTL to remove the soothing balm of Euronews, so we couldn't keep up with her statuesque public appearances dwarfing her mini-Gaulle lover, that short-arse, what's his name? President of France. Yeah, him.

Miss Carla Gilberta Bruni Tedeschi: young, bright, Italian and heiress to a tyre manufacturing fortune has always done what she liked. You want to be a model? Check. Upgrade that status to supermodel? Qui, no problem, my sweetness. Chanteuse/enchantress of languid folk ballads? Why not? The Queen of the French political elite? Done. What's left? Queen for real, maybe? Swift return of the monarchy, off with their heads, music festivals at Versailles – remember, she can do whatever she wants.

When Carla had a fling with Mick Jagger, Jerry Hall can't have been overjoyed. Other girlfriends of Jagger's over the years were content to remain just that, but Carla wanted more. Carla always wants more. She also went out with God himself, Eric Clapton, but Carla was never content to just be the pretty face beside these rock Gods. An accomplished musician and singer herself, she always considered herself their equal and we have to admit, she has a point. She dated former French Socialist Prime Minister Laurence Fabius, tycoon Donald Trump, publisher (and philosopher no less) Jean-Paul Enthoven and then his son, Raphael with whom she had a son, thus proving that French people really do have as complicated love lives as their loquacious films suggest.[72] She was famously quoted by Le Figaro proclaiming "I am faithful.?.?. to myself! I am monogamous from time to time but I prefer polygamy and polyandry [its female equivalent]."[73] What a rock star. The refreshing thing is that in her high profile relationships with high-powered men, she's done it on her own terms (the independent wealth helps here) and with such insouciance, that's she's not demonised for it the way many women are dealt with by the tabloids.

Carla has managed to convince the world that it was the diminutive dynamo French President who seduced her and not the reverse. Sarkozy thought he devastated her with his charisma and dominated her with his gallic charm, but Carla's seduction technique is arachnoid in its deadliness. Poor little blighter never stood a chance.

So Carla Bruni-Sarkozy wants to see Lisbon ratified and the reforms pressed on with, so her grand place at the heart of Europe and France topples Josephine in the minds of political love historians. If Carla thinks Lisbon is a good thing, let's go with it and hope she's still living in the Elysée Palace by the autumn, so that we can glimpse the future of Europe caught in the flash of her cats' eyes.

TL: Alas, no protocol prevents Carla from annexing the rest of Europe with her charm.

72   *The Independent on Sunday*, 18 December 2007
73   *The Telegraph*, 11 Jan 2008

61 Other states' sympathy with Ireland's concerns is finite.

All the other Member States have ratified Lisbon according to their own constitutional requirements, bar Germany, Poland and the Czech Republic.

Germany's parliament have already ratified Lisbon and following legal challenges, the German Constitutional Court ruled that Lisbon was compatible with German law, but suspended ratification until extra German law had been drafted to ensure the level of national parliamentary participation that Lisbon called for. Poland's President Lech Kaczynski is delaying signing it through until Ireland votes Yes, as he views it as 'pointless' to do so until then. In May, the Czech Parliament voted Lisbon through. Following the collapse of the government, their Eurosceptic President Vaclac Klaus is also waiting to see how the autumn referendum here goes, before he signs the Czech ratification.

The highlight of thirty-six years of Irish membership has to be the day of the welcomes in 2004, when twenty-seven Heads of State gathered at Áras an Úachtarán to formally embrace the ten accession States of the Czech Republic, Slovakia, Slovenia, Hungary, Poland, Estonia, Latvia, Lithuania, Cyprus and Malta.

This 'big bang' enlargement was a bold jump forward for the Union whose five-year anniversary this year marked significant improvement in the fortunes of these States, but uncertain times ahead. Trade between the original EU15 and EU27 in the period 1999 to 2007 went from €177 billion to €500 billion. Economic migrants travelling from Poland, Latvia and

Lithuania to Ireland have had an overwhelmingly positive effect for us and them. No one foresaw how many temporary workers would want to come to Ireland. In all, some 5 per cent of the working age population here last year came from the EU10 countries, a figure far higher than any other EU State.[74]

We've served as a role model for these mainly Eastern European States who saw that a small State could wield influence that belied its economic power and size of population. They saw the benefits to Ireland's economy and wanted to achieve the same things for their own citizens. They see the boom years as evidence of the EU's impact on Ireland, frequently forgetting to factor in the recession here in the 1980s – if there is a lesson, it's that it takes time to integrate into the Common Market and fully absorb the infrastructural investment.

> If we think we are now all of a sudden ill-equipped to deal with a global financial crisis of this magnitude on our own, you wonder how Slovakia or Estonia might feel?

These states haven't had the benefit of thirty-six years of membership and concomitant EU investment in infrastructure and training. They desperately need the reform of the institutions to go ahead after seven years of discussion. If we think we are now all of a sudden ill-equipped to deal with a global financial crisis of this magnitude on our own, you wonder how Slovakia or Estonia might feel? Hungary and Latvia are in the grip of the worst recession they've experienced in twenty years, encountering the credit and property bubbles we're only too familiar with. There have been violent clashes between pro-

74   Ruadhan Mac Cormaic/Paul Gillespie, *The Irish Times*, 2 May 2009

testers and police there, in Lithuania and Bulgaria with demonstrations against their governments' handling of the economic crisis (the Bulgarians joined with Romania in January 2007). Latvia has asked the IMF if the terms of its bailout deal can be amended to allow for a larger deficit as bankruptcy looms. We have been consistently adept at forging alliances with recently joined members in the aftermath of previous EU enlargements. With Croatia hoping to join by 2010, a rejection of Lisbon would lessen Ireland's ability to build alliances with new Member States.

Montenegro and Albania have both applied to be part of the Union joining Turkey and Croatia in the queue. Iceland could be on a fast-track negotiation that would see it join with Croatia. If the established States view further negotiation on Lisbon to be a waste of time given a second rejection by Ireland, the Union will revert to an intergovernmental system. The larger States will seek arrangements between themselves leaving out smaller States like the weaker of the 12 new Members and also ourselves now we're tagged with the reputation of being self-destructively obstructionist and economically cracked. So it is perfectly reasonable that a cry in answer to UKIP's cynical 'Respect the Irish Vote' would come from the States who've ratified Lisbon – 'respect our right to move ahead without you'. Whether that is stated explicitly or manifests itself as an undercurrent of influence and access loss for Ireland, it is likely that States will be pragmatic about their own futures within the EU and regret it as they pass us by, but bypass us nonetheless.

TL: we're the only obstacle to ratification

62 The European Investment Bank has a €300 million loan fund for small business.

The European Investment Bank was created by the Treaty of Rome as the long-term lending institution to the EU. In March 2009, it announced a €300 million fund that could assist Irish Small-to-Medium Enterprises (SMEs). The funds are in addition to the €50 million it made available to Bank of Scotland (Ireland) for investment to SMEs.

The EIB made loans of up to €57 billion across Europe in 2008. The Investment Bank has thus lent out €350 billion in total since its inception.

Three Irish banks – Bank of Ireland, Allied Irish Bank and Ulster Bank – are acting as intermediaries and lend the money to projects that 'further EU policy objectives'. With Ireland opting out of the €200 billion European Economic Recovery Plan, as its pursuing its own policies to stimulate growth and demand, while trying to stem the haemorrhaging of the public finances, it's all the more important to have this extra stream of money available for investment.

Patricia Callan, the Director of the Small Firms Association applauded the move. It also gave her the golden opportunity to clap herself on the back for a herculean lobbying effort. She said "The EIB finance adds to the positive engagements that SFA have held with An Tánaiste, as well as direct meetings with all the major financial institutions and the recently announced Code of Conduct for Business Lending."[75] This natural ability

---

75   www.finfacts.ie, 24 April 2009

to make fair comment, while also justifying her own existence, speaks of a golden future in politics.

It's all very well for such moves to be announced, but the proof of the pudding will be if those bastard, greedy Irish banks actually give up some of the cash to the SMEs instead of hoarding it for themselves.

Displaying some pretty well-developed self-congratulatory nous himself, EIB President Philippe Maystadt pointed out how speedily the EIB had acted without overstretching itself and said "Although we cannot work miracles on our own, the EIB stands at the service of Europe, and will continue to play a strong and active role in spurring economic recovery." The EIB has provided loans in Ireland for some larger infrastructural projects like the ESB transmission and distribution networks, the Biomedical Sciences Research Centre in Trinity College Dublin and the second Terminal at Dublin Airport.[76]

> ...the proof of the pudding will be if those bastard, greedy Irish banks actually give up some of the cash to the SMEs instead of hoarding it for themselves.

A yes to Lisbon also means that Irish businesses can cut out the middlemen of the Irish banks and apply directly to the EIB, because of a change in the EIB statute in the Treaty. Simon Carswell, financial correspondent at the Irish Times did however tell us that "The European Investment Bank is just a drop in the ocean as to the amount of credit that the Irish economy needs. It's helpful, but it's not nearly enough."

---

76   www.irelandforeurope.ie

Apparently lending from the EIB is done on very favourable terms due to its AAA credit rating. *100 Reasons* wishes we had an AAA credit rating. *100 Reasons* also wonders if one were to lie about it, would one nonchalantly drop into conversation 'Well actually, I'm A-A-A on the old credit rating stakes these days', or would 'Meant to mention, I'm Triple-A certified, by the way' sound better? Triple trips off the tongue more smoothly, definitely, so we'll slick back the hair, get all suited and booted and go with that one.

TL: 249A TFEU The words European Investment Bank do appear in the Treaty, but it's very much a recurring cameo.

Lisbon provides for the accession of the Union to the ECHR. The legal basis is established in Article 6 of the Lisbon Treaty for the EU to accede to the European Convention for the Protection of Human Rights and Fundamental Freedoms (ECHR). The ECHR was signed under the aegis of the Council of Europe in 1950 setting out the standards for fundamental civic and political rights and the institutions to protect them like the European Court of Human Rights in Strasbourg.

The rights guaranteed by the Convention include freedom of thought, conscience and religion, freedom of expression, right to life, right to marry, freedom of assembly and association, right to respect for private and family life, right to liberty and security, right to a fair trial, no punishment without law, prohibition of torture, prohibition of slavery and forced labour, right to an effective remedy and prohibition of discrimination. Further rights are set out in protocols attached to the ECHR.

It also means that the actions of the Union and the European Court of Justice can be examined by the independent European Court of Human Rights.

It also means that the actions of the Union and the European Court of Justice can be examined by the independent European Court of Human Rights. If a European citizen thought his or her rights had been violated and they had run out of options for redress in their home country, they could petition the court in Strasbourg. States can also bring their case against another State to the court. So while the Member States of the EU are all also members of the convention, now EU law must also be underpinned by the provisions of the ECHR.

It strengthens protections by submitting the EU's legal procedures to independent scrutiny. It is the shoring up of a potential legal loophole whereby the EU's laws might not have been subject to the same rigorous examination as that of the national laws of its Members. In the words of the Convention Working Group, this is intended to "give a strong political signal of the coherence between the Union and the 'greater Europe' reflected in the Council of Europe and its pan- European human rights system."[77]

It will put pressure on more recent signatories of the ECHR like Bulgaria (1992), the Czech Republic (1993), Slovakia (1993), Slovenia (1994), Romania (1994) and Latvia (1997) to make sure that no human rights violators slip through their nets. This combined with the Charter of Fundamental Rights and the social clause tightens up social and human rights protection across the EU.

TL: Article 6 TEU

---

[77]   Government White Paper on the Lisbon Treaty 2009, DFA, July 2009, pg. 34

64 National vetoes are protected.

National parliaments have a veto and six months to use it on any move from unanimity voting to QMV.

Upon being notified that the European Council is considering a change from unanimity to Qualified Majority Voting (QMV), any single national parliament can object within six months, thus also holding a veto over such a decision.

This is the mechanism of giving ample notice of any intention of the European Council to use the provisions allowing for the simplified revision of certain aspects of the Treaties relating to voting in the Council of Ministers and extension of the co-decision procedure between the European Parliament and the Council.

National parliaments are to be given at least six months' notice of any intention by the European Council to make certain limited adjustments to the voting rules in the Treaties – under a simplified revision procedure, known as the 'general passerelle' arrangement. Any move by the European Council to allow decisions previously determined unanimously to be made by QMV, or to extend the co-decision procedure between the Council and the European Parliament, can be blocked by a single national parliament or by a single Government.

As a further safeguard, any future changes to the Treaties involving new competences for the Union would be examined by a Convention in which the National Parliaments would be strongly represented.

TL: Protocol on the role of National Parliaments in the European Union

65 If you vote yes to Lisbon it'll piss off Declan Ganley.

Ganley's the British/Irish millionaire defence contractor and dilettante politician who was behind and in front of the Libertas No campaign. He failed in his bid to be elected as an MEP for Ireland North-West and conceded that he could neither lead Libertas nor a No campaign if he couldn't get elected himself. He has bowed out of politics.

The leader of Libertas has been under unwaveringly suspicious scrutiny by the Irish media since he made an impact by running a No campaign in the first referendum. Ganley's company, Rivada Networks, supply telecommunications equipment for disaster relief and defence capabilities. Bush's former telecommunications advisor John Kneuer is senior Vice-President of the company. The presence of top-brass US military figures like Admiral Timothy J. Keating, head of the US Pacific Command, Admiral James L. Loy, formerly the first deputy secretary of Homeland Security and Lt. General Dennis McCarthy, ex-director of operations for the US Atlantic Command on the boards of his companies do not dissipate the dark whisperings of CIA connections.[78]

Perhaps they're all being unfair to him and it's an invented story like 'Al Gore the Exaggerator' during the 2000 US Presidential election. Al didn't lie about his part in championing internet development or that the writer of *Love Story* based the hero on him, but it didn't matter. The media just didn't like the man and ran with the non-story until it died, was resuscitated, died again, ad infinitum. Maybe Ganley isn't the shadowy fig-

---

78   David McKittrick, *The Independent* (UK) 10 June 2008

ure he was portrayed as. Maybe they just don't like the dude. There's a lot to be jealous of: the €300 million personal fortune, the snappy one-liners (sorry that was Michael O'Leary, keep getting mixed up), the €300 million personal fortune, the snappy dressing (sorry, that was Denis O'Brien), the €300 million personal fortune,[79] the gravitas (sorry, that was Feargal Quinn). It's really down to transparency – no one knows exactly how Ganley became such a wealthy man. Sometimes it's a great plus for a multi-millionaire to enter politics, as they can't be accused of getting into it for the money, but it helps if the public are familiar with how the money was made.

He spent €40 million running 532 candidates across Europe and only one, French MEP Phillipe de Villiers, got in...

Minister of State Dick Roche had great fun winding him up on the *News at One* by accusing him of 'wrapping himself in the tricolour' whenever it suited him and then the *Irish Times* pointed out he'd registered as a British citizen on official UK companies documents up until 2006. The authenticity test is something all politicians identifying with a particular area must wrestle with. Now no one ever accused Declan of having a Tuam accent, but Ganley's Hiberno-English sometimes veered towards the Kiwi and while you've kids from Donegal with mid-Atlantic drawls from watching too much of *The Hills*, if you're from Dundalk say, you had better have a Dundalk accent, if you're going to run for the town council.

Ganley attempted to launch Libertas as a pan-European party under the tutelage of his Danish mentor Jans-Peter Bonde, the

---

79   *Time Magazine*, 15 April 2009

founder of the other major No to Lisbon organisation, Intergroup SOS Democracy and drafted in Lynton Crosby, the Australian election campaign svengali. It didn't work to a rather devastating degree. He spent €40 million running 532 candidates across Europe and only one, French MEP Phillipe de Villiers, got in, quickly confirming he was no longer a member of the organisation.[80]

Declan may have bowed out of fronting a No campaign, but it's not the last we've seen of Declan Ganley.

TL: There's no part of the Lisbon Treaty that Ganley relates to.

---

80   *Irish Independent*, 30 June 2009

66 Lisbon protects schools & hospitals from takeover by greedy capitalists.

The Protocol on Services of General Interest guarantees States' ability to fund & run education & health sector as they see fit and clarifies that national, regional and local authorities have wide discretion as to how they organise public services.

As a result of Lisbon, there will be no fast food-branded private schools with morning assembly replaced with a short message from our sponsors...

The Protocol states *the provisions of the Treaties do not affect in any way the competence of Member States to provide, commission and organise non-economic services of general interest.*

That's about as clear as you can possibly be.

It also mentions the local bodies where responsibilty for the provision of these services should reside, stating the EU recognises that *the essential role and the wide discretion of national, regional and local authorities in providing, commissioning and organising services of general economic interest as closely as possible to the needs of the users.*

Not only that, but the Council meeting of Heads of States in December 2008 re-confirmed the responsibility of Member States for the delivery of education and health services.

Foreign Affairs Minister Micheál Martin, in response to claims that Health and Education services are at risk, said that "the claim that these services will end up being 'traded like sacks of spuds' is ridiculous."

This is the last remaining plank of Sinn Féin's argument against the Treaty, which is surprising as current educational policy is reinforced by the legal guarantees. In the section dealing with the Right to Life, Family and Education, it stated that nothing in the Treaties affected *the protection of the rights in respect of education in Articles 42 and 44.2.4 and 44.2.5 provided by the Constitution of Ireland.*

As a result of Lisbon, there will be no fast food-branded private schools with morning assembly replaced with a short message from our sponsors, no in-classroom commercial screens and no teachers teaching an alternative history of Europe where the EU was founded by benevolent multinationals to spread the gospel of 'earn and consume'. That's all waiting for them on telly, when they get home. The people we have to blame for the relentless encroachment of capitalist enterprise into our lives are ourselves, as we vote for the big name market leaders everyday, with our wallets.

TL: Article 16 [14] TFEU; Protocol on Services of General Interest

67 Euronews is mesmerising entertainment, even if you're only slightly stoned.

Ah, Euronews. The faintest whisper of the theme music is valium to the ears. It's news without the stress – there's no concept of time here – things happen in a haze somewhere in Mittel-Europe sometime last week.

Social unrest, plane crashes and earthquakes are all filtered through the prism of how well the EU's agencies can cope with social unrest, plane crashes and earthquakes. It's reality for optimists, who like to learn three things an hour that'll make them feel better about humanity. Sky is all tabloid nonsense-panic whipped up by Stepford news anchors or frothy items on premieres from Leicester Square, sports rows or weather forecasts from which you retain nothing bar an appreciation/burning lust for ladies' gym-toned calf muscles. BBC is serious coverage of serious issues for serious people who had best be British to really care about the serious issues aired. Euronews is a realist's view of Utopia: an idyll studded with surmountable problems.

Before Euronews, did you ever stop to consider that the letters making up the word news were also the first letters of each direction? As they swirl around North, South, East and West, it becomes obvious that the people behind Euronews are very clever indeed.

Those 'no comment' sections – news that's actually soothing – no editorial judgment imposed from on high (apart from deciding where to point the camera, of course), no jabbering narration and, in its place, birdsong; that addictive clarinet (or is it an oboe?) refrain when the weather is on that improves your pub quiz geographical knowledge with each serving; le Mag & Rendez-vous arts segments showcasing Estonian shock sculpture installations, Viennese political dance festivals and Danish poetry-slam shows you'll never attend, but always feel you could and would enjoy if you did.[81]

Propaganda from the EU? Perhaps, but it seems benign, includes coverage of any anti-EU dissent and strikes such a note of cultured urbanity that the thought that one was being manipulated into being pro-European seems about as insidious as an elderly aunt's drive to help one appreciate opera or improve one's table manners.

Its inclusiveness not only draws the heathens into High Culture, but the aspirant countries like Croatia and Montenegro are covered along with the countries in the European Neighbourhood Policy like Moldova, the Ukraine and beyond. Borat may not have been too kind to places like these, but Euronews is always ready with the tale of the local classical pianist who's weighing up a career in music with his responsibilities to family, community and his studies in bio-physics. The only threatening part of it all is the implicit message to old Europe – these people are bright, talented and have worryingly good posture – work harder, if you don't want to end up cleaning their pool.

TL: Euronews is not in the Lisbon Treaty, but the Lisbon Treaty is in Euronews.

---

81   *100 Reasons* wishes to point out that these swirly, chilled, respite-from-life sections are in no way more enjoyable under the influence of any substance stronger than coffee. Euronews is narcotic enough.

68 Lisbon has nothing to do with tax.

The European Commission's consideration of a Common Consolidated Corporate Tax Base has nothing to do with the Lisbon Treaty.

In fact, the legal guarantee that Ireland secured from Europe states *Nothing in the Treaty of Lisbon makes any change of any kind, for any member state, to the extent or operation of the competence of the European Union in relation to taxation.*

The Irish Taxation Institute (ITI) confirmed that the European Commission's long-term consideration of a Common Consolidated Corporate Tax Base (CCCTB) and the Lisbon Treaty were entirely separate issues and should not be linked. Therefore, ratification of the Lisbon Treaty would not lead to the automatic introduction of the CCCTB.

The idea behind the CCCTB would be to consolidate the income of corporations operating in the EU on which the Member States can levy tax. This is very different to the concept of tax harmonisation which means one rate of tax across the EU. So firstly, the CCCTB does not mean tax harmonisation and secondly, Ireland retains a veto over proposals such as the CCCTB and this will not change.

The Irish Taxation Institute also clearly state that Ireland's 12.5 per cent corporation tax rate and other direct taxation measures are safe and that the Government would retain control over direct taxation policy.

Throughout the 2008 campaign, Sinn Féin (ex-)MEP Mary Lou MacDonald insisted on bringing up the 'distortion of competition' principle as the mechanism that would negate our unanimity on the corporation tax issue. This is totally refuted by the Commission President. "...the distortion of competition is not put as a principle against the rule of unanimity for tax matters. On the contrary, it is something that is added and this is the general rule in Europe as you know."[82]

ITI (again boringly the Irish Tax Institute and not the Irish Theatre Institute who have unfortunately nothing to add to the CCCTB debate) is similarly unequivocal as to what Lisbon means to Irish tax policy. "The terms of the Lisbon Treaty presented no threat to our ability to control our own destiny regarding our corporation tax rates. Ireland's veto on tax changes is intact and copperfastened."[83]

Labour TD Ruairi Quinn, who was the Minister for Finance with the Rainbow coalition that actually introduced the 12.5 per cent corporate tax rate that has been so fundamental in encouraging inward investment, says "neither enhanced cooperation nor this Treaty could leave a back door open to a Common Consolidated Corporate Tax Base (CCCTB)." Quinn points out that the UK and Slovakia have also been vocal opponents of the CCCTB. Germany now also believes tax harmonisation and common EU taxes as 'unworkable' and 'politically unfeasible.'[84]

Dick Roche pithily puts it "If there's anything that would bore the pants off the ordinary citizen, it's that type of debate."

TL: there is no mention of direct taxation in the Lisbon Treaty.

---

82   Barroso, NFE Plenary Sessions, pg. 233
83   Sub-Ctte Report on Ireland's Future in the EU, Nov. 2008, pg. 36
84   Ruairi Quinn's speech to the Small Firms Association, IBEC

69 It'll improve our reputation in Europe.

The Lisbon issue dominates how other Member States think of Ireland and our negotiating power is damaged as a result.

In 2008, Ambassador Bobby McDonagh, the Permanent Representative of Ireland to the EU said "Until earlier this year, people, on meeting an Irish representative, would mentally think of Ireland as a small constructive country which has been helpful to them and so they wished only to be helpful to us. Now, without any ill-will, when they see us they think of Lisbon. It is like a light bulb flashing over our heads."[85]

Until this veil/light bulb/very bad stench of distrustworthiness and downright self-disgust can be lifted from over our furrowed brows, we're 'Res Publica Non Grata' in Europe...

Ambassador Bobby must be sick of glancing up to see himself bathed halo-like in the non-celestial light of political suspicion, confusion and economic doom. It must be a blue-greenish light like the type you feel shimmering on your greasy, grey skin when you're a bit pissed and you decide that a spot of 4AM grocery shopping in the 24-hour Tesco is a good idea.

With the Lisbon issue pushing all others out to the side for our fellow EU Members when it comes to Ireland, it is harder for us to contribute our views to the policy debates within the institu-

---

85   Sub-Ctte Report on Ireland's Future in the EU, Nov. 2008, pg. 24

tions. Ireland is no longer looked upon as a flexible negotiator or compromise builder. It's not even viewed as a constructive Member anymore. It's viewed with pity and disappointment that such a promising young economy could screw it all up quite so conclusively. Until this veil/light bulb/very bad stench of distrustworthiness and downright self-disgust can be lifted from over our furrowed brows, we're 'Res Publica Non Grata' in Europe and we've got to turn that around starting with Lisbon and then slowly rebuild respect for Ireland from there. It's going to take a while.

"The No vote has sent a strongly negative signal of intent not only to our European counterparts but also to the many multinational companies which locate in Ireland because of the access our location and our participation in EU affairs give to Europe's 460 million consumers."[86]

So says Paul Rellis. He's the Managing Director of Microsoft Ireland and President of the American Chamber of Commerce in Ireland. He knows a thing or two about the reality of foreign direct investment in Ireland.

TL: the Microsoft warning does not appear in the Treaty, but does it need to?

---

86   Sub-Ctte Report on Ireland's Future in the EU, Nov. 2008, pg. 29

70 Even the naysayers say Yes to Lisbon II.

A leading member of the No Campaign Naoise Nunn now believes we don't have the luxury of a second No vote.

The most entertaining spat between ex-Libertasers so far has been Declan Ganley's denunciation of Naoise Nunn (excuse the nun), after his ex-executive director switched to supporting the Treaty.

Nunn told the *Irish Times* the reasons for his change of heart: "The circumstances have changed: internationally, economically, financially and domestically. We don't have the luxury of doing anything else. I am glad that we had a referendum. We were the only Member State to do so, to have a proper debate, or something like a proper debate."

Naoise Nunn was widely credited with being the brains behind the successful billboard campaign which played on fears of what would happen if Ireland lost a permanent position on the Commission. "But it appears that that issue has been resolved, or, at least, there is a serious will to resolve it," he said in reference to the agreement EU leaders came to last December commiting to retaining one Commissioner per State that has since been legally guaranteed.

Ganley denied his ex-employee's claims of "scaremongering and misinformation" on both sides of the campaign, saying "that's Fianna Fáil language if ever I heard it... we pointed out the facts." His old boss claimed that Nunn "was now working for Fianna Fáil as a consultant." Nunn is actually working for suicidally outspoken former Minister for State John McGuinness, not Fianna Fáil directly. As it's indeed doubtful how much longer McGuinness himself will choose to work for the Soldiers of Destiny as he keeps publicly and justifiably attacking his own ex-boss, Tánaiste Mary Coughlan, it's pushing it to say Nunn's on the FF payroll.

Minister for Foreign Affairs Micheál Martin welcomed Mr Nunn's change of heart.

"I think it is significant that a person who was very much involved in the No Campaign on the last occasion has come forward to say he believes it is in the best interests of Ireland now to ratify Lisbon when it comes before the people again."

Nunn predicted a positive result in any forthcoming referendum, saying a No vote would be "dangerous for the country, but I don't think frankly that that is going to happen."[87]

Naoise Nunn continues to run his live political forum *Leviathan,* which gathers politicians, business leaders and journalists to debate the issues with satirical and comedic interludes, so it'll be interesting to see what debate on a Lisbon theme surfaces from the deep in the Button Factory or other venues in the run-up to the referendum on October 2.

TL: Libertas and Lisbon are mutually exclusive: their bits never touch.

---

87   Mark Hennessy, *The Irish Times,* 28 April 2009

71 Ireland has suffered economically directly from its rejection of Lisbon.

Yes, yes, this one is a little tough to prove. In June 2008, Ireland rejected the Lisbon Treaty by the narrowest of margins and over the next year or so, the Irish economy fell to shit. It would be churlish to lump all of our woes into the doom bucket of our slackening relationship with the EU, but it's an element.

Instead, *100 Reasons* must factor in the worst global recession in living memory, Bertie's legacy and the shower of fuckwits currently running the Irish Government.

Professor John Fitzgerald of the Economic and Social Research Institute (ESRI) believes that the measures dealing with the banking crisis have been affected by our blackened reputation in Europe after shooting down Lisbon I.

"The extension of the bank guarantee to the non-Irish banks on competition grounds was spurious. Already Irish banks were facing competition from Northern Rock, which had a full British government guarantee. Since the introduction of the Irish guarantee the UK government has become the largest shareholder in Ulster Bank. All of these changes, which were fully justified because of the financial crisis, affected competition. Yet the EU Commission did not seek to intervene."

Fitzgerald thinks that the Commission would have weighed in, if Ireland was in a position of better standing vis-à-vis the nature of our future involvement in Europe.

"The EU Commission would most likely not have got involved

in the Irish case were it not for the fact that the UK, Germany and France were already aggrieved at Ireland's position on Lisbon. The extension of the guarantee to non-Irish banks potentially increases Ireland's contingent liabilities by €40 billion. While unlikely to be called, this guarantee has a significant price in increasing risk, and hence the cost of borrowing for the State. It also increases uncertainty about the Irish economy, with potentially adverse effects on investment."[88]

It's hard to call. If we're to believe one of the celebrity economists we're inclined to trust occasionally, David McWilliams, who wonders why we would ever trust the ESRI again after they had failed to predict the current crisis. So who's to know? Well you would think, the guys and girls who are paid to take educated guesses on these things... One thing's for sure, when you're a small, open economy reliant on our exports of goods, people and services (especially financial & ICT) on the one hand and foreign direct investment on the other in the middle of a global financial shitfest, you had better have powerful friends and if not quite that, then mildly benevolent allies. Britain? The US? They've got their own problems.

TL: the wheels on Dublin Bus go round and round, until the wheels come off and we discover that all the bus routes have been cut under a part-Green Party Government: we're skint, folks.

---

88   Sub-Ctte Report on Ireland's Future in the EU, Nov. 2008, pg. 24

72 Any social legislation worth a tuppenny damn came out of the EU.

The big one was equal pay for men and women in 1974 that came in with the Anti-Discrimination Act. It's pretty easy for young Irish women today to choose not to be feminists, as all the major battles were won for them by their mothers. It's less attractive for girls nowadays to embrace an ideology that has been attacked for so many years that many of the slurs have stuck. Michael D. Higgins told us "I do wonder sometimes when our society would have stopped demanding our daughters to retire from their jobs to take care of the home and children upon marriage if our membership of the EU together will certain outstanding individuals like Mary Robinson had not sped up reform in this area."

Social legislation like equal rights for part-time workers with pro-rata pay, equal pay for fixed-term workers and the Working Time directive have all originated in the EU. The latter limits the 7-day working week to 48 hours with proper rest periods, although this still appears to be news to the HSE if its continued treatment of junior doctors and thus the patients, is anything to go by, exposing it to continuing sanction from the Commission. This directive also guaranteed workers to 4 weeks paid holiday a year. The European Trade Union Confederation recently secured equal rights for agency workers. With regard to maternity rights, EU legislation guarantees that women cannot be validly dismissed if they get up knocked up. Women are now entitled to a minimum of 14 weeks maternity leave. Irish periods of maternity leave - 26 weeks paid and up to 16 weeks unpaid - are in fact higher than the EU average. Unfortunately, no matter how much sensitive Neo-Nu-new men cry and whinge and 'empathise', they still aren't allowed doss around the house and watch for the duration of the baby holiday.

The signing of the Charter of Social Rights in 1989 is what kicked off what has become known as the European Social Model. Legislation on working time, parental level, equal pay, the protection of young workers, health and safety in the work-place, greater equality, social security, anti-discrimination and workers rights have been enacted. EU social legislation helps workers by making qualifications transferable from Member State to Member State, coordinates social security schemes so workers are entitled to unemployment benefit wherever they are should they lose their jobs, ensures better working condi-tions, enforces equality between men and women, races and people of different sexuality.

Proinsias de Rossa chooses the 2000 directive tackling dis-crimination in the workplace on the grounds of disability, age, religion or belief, and sexual orientation as one of the most important pieces of social legislation. "This was one of the first directives adopted under the anti-discrimination Article #13 negotiated to the treaties by the Rainbow Coalition. The EU is currently in the process of adopting legislation tackling dis-crimination on these grounds 'beyond' the workplace, i.e. in the provision of services such as health and education, etc."

Blair Horan, the General Secretary of the Civil Public and Serv-ices Union says "Being at the heart of the European Union is central from our point of view. I cannot conceive of any sig-nificant item of workers' rights legislation in the last thirty-five years that has not emanated from the Union, starting with the equal pay legislation.

TL: Article 6 TEU: Charter of Fundamental Rights

73 The Lisbon Treaty is an organic extension of the Union.

The new Treaty builds on the existing European Union and the treaties that underpin it.

> ...tacking on our innovations by means of post-its, tipp-ex and sticky tape to create a labyrinthine interweaving of all the Treaties to date on documents dating back to 1957.

The failed Constitutional Treaty would have abolished all existing treaties and re-founded the Union. Abolish all the Treaties? Crazy talk. Why would you construct one comprehensive, easy-to-read Treaty containing all the rules of the EU, when you could just lash all the amendments and protocols you needed into the existing treaties making the whole thing well nigh incomprehensible to the layman?

Well you see, they tried the former method with the Constitutional Treaty, but voters were confused with their politicians expressing complex ideas in a lucid way and being thoroughly transparent. So now we're back to the old way of tacking on our innovations by means of post-its, tipp-ex and sticky tape to create a labyrinthine interweaving of all the Treaties to date on documents dating back to 1957. The main thing that is discarded from the Constitutional Treaty by Lisbon, is, well, the Constitution. Constitution meant a superstate and an unreadable Treaty meant business-as-usual.

TL: the whole kit and kaboodle.

74 There is no mention of conscription or of an EU army in the Lisbon Treaty.

Did the bogus fears of conscription to a European army come out of the 'scaremongering and misinformation' that Naoise Nunn accused both sides of during the 2008 campaign? Did it emanate from No Campaign push-polling on the doorsteps or over the phone lines?

'Question 19: If you were told that by voting *Yes* for Lisbon it would lead to conscription and a pan-European military force, would you be less likely to vote *Yes* for the Treaty?'

That's an example of a push-poll that may or may not have happened. It's a lovely import from the US that folds scurrilous ideas into the form of a question, thus putting it in the voter's head without having actually stated it as a fact.

Or if you want to be drawn into conspiracy theory territory, let's go! Perhaps this alleged strategy was introduced by the Yes side as a stick to beat the No Campaign with. Ah hah! Create the dirty trick to complain about dirty tricks. Anything's possible. Let's just put this to rest, shall we?

Along with Sweden, Austria, Cyprus and Malta, Finland is another neutral EU Member State. The Finnish Foreign Minister Alexander Stubb says "The EU is not a military alliance and decisions on defence matters remain sovereign decisions of the individual Member States."[89]

89   Sub-Ctte Report on Ireland's Future in the EU, Nov. 2008, pg. 49

So no, we're not going to send our 19-year-olds on year-long military service learning to shoot guns when they should just be shooting their mouths off, we're not going to send them to Iraq or Afghanistan, we're not even going to send them to the Curragh if they tend to get spooked by horses and don't want to go.

> ...we're not going to send our 19-year-olds on year-long military service learning to shoot guns when they should just be shooting their mouths off...

The Seville Declarations of 2002 noted that the Treaty on European Union *does not impose any binding mutual defence commitments. Nor does the development of the Union's capacity to conduct humanitarian and crisis management tasks involve the establishment of a European army.* The Lisbon Treaty retains this.

The legal guarantees secured by Biffo state the Treaty of Lisbon does not provide for the creation of a European army or for conscription to any military formation.

Conscription of EU citizens is a total fabrication made up by scary people to scare people, because it's one of the scariest ideas we can think of.

TL: No conscription in here.

75 Enhances the legitimate role of unions in EU development

Article 152 establishes the Tripartite Social Summit for Growth and Employment.

Selfishly, 100 Reasons advocates moving to Sweden, marrying a buxom ice-blond snow queen and availing of and gorging upon as many Swedish clichés it can...

The Union recognises and promotes the role of the social partners at its level, taking into account the diversity of national systems. It shall facilitate dialogue between the social partners respecting their autonomy.

Former Fine Gael MEP John Cushnahan pointed out that in tandem with the new social clause, Article 152 goes on to make provision for social dialogue and recognises the social partners.[90]

This was a clause insisted on by the European Trade Union Congress. It also establishes the Tripartite Social Summit for Growth and Employment that aims to contribute to social dialogue.

These measures taken together with the Charter for Fundamental Rights significantly reinforce the European Social Model and the EU's commitment to safeguarding the rights and opportunities of its workers.

---

90   97th plenary session, NFE, 15 May 2008

Ex-Labour Party leader Ruairi Quinn believes that "This Treaty, more so than any other piece of European legislation in its history, enshrines social protection into the very core of all the Union's activities."[91]

Quinn believes that countries do not have to face a stark choice between open market capitalism and a high level of social protection, but that we can have both pressures tempering one another as is institutionalised in the Nordic countries. Selfishly, *100 Reasons* advocates moving to Sweden, marrying a buxom ice-blond snow queen and availing of and gorging upon as many Swedish clichés it can sit in, touch, watch, fit in its mouth, drink and swallow. However, it must concede that perhaps a more mature/less morally corrupt plan would be to take the best elements of Sweden's style, recreation and of course, social economy and put them into action here. A hard lifetime's work to change Ireland for the better or a cheap flight to bliss, carrying one's transferable skills and worldly assets in a rattly plastic bag. It's a tough call alright.

TL: Title IX [X] Article 136A [152] TFEU

---

91   97th plenary session, NFE, 15 May 2008

76 A rejection of Lisbon puts an indefinite hold on any further enlargement.

Olli Rehn, the EU Enlargement Minister, is trying to pretend that it's business as usual. He's trying to convince the politicians and the public that enlargement policy is not a reason for the institutional and economic problems facing the EU. The Finnish Commissioner is managing the accession talks for Turkey and Croatia at the moment and says that locking the barn door now risks destabilising the Balkan states like Bosnia, Serbia, Macedonia and Montenegro who also desperately want and need to join the EU.

Both Nicolas Sarkozy and Angela Merkel have threatened to block further enlargement pending a decision on Lisbon. The French President said "It is certain that as long as we have not solved the institutional problem, the question of enlargement is stopped de jure or de facto." He argues that under the current system, it is impossible for the EU to function properly with twenty-seven members, let alone bringing more into the fold. Merkel's Christian Democrats party (CDU) calls for a "phase of consolidation, during which a consolidation of the EU's values and institutions should take priority over further enlargement."[92] The CDUs like the word consolidation. They also like to sing *99 Red Balloons* in the shower. (Only joking, I've no idea what Christian Democrats like to sing in the shower, maybe something by The Christians or Kraftwerk or David Hasselhoff.) Anyway the mainstays of the EU are viewing the stretch marks on the EU's belly and no amount of bio-oil seems to shift them. They aren't that keen on jumping back

---

92   Jamie Smyth, *The Irish Times*, 2 May 2009

in the sack quite so soon after delivering a litter of twelve new EU babies in close succession.

The UK is a traditional supporter of enlargement, despite anti-EU campaigns in recent years by the Tories. However, Gordon Brown's ill-judged rabble-rousing phrase 'British Jobs for British People' promptly decorated placards in wildcat protests outside the Lindsey oil refinery and elsewhere, so British support for further EU enlargement at the moment would be political suicide.

Albania has joined the queue of Croatia, Turkey and Montenegro. Iceland is considering whether to avail of Olli Rehn's fast-track accession with Croatia as early as 2011. Bosnia and Serbia have signed stabilisation and association agreements with a further trade agreement between the Serbs and the EU. These are the first steps towards applying for full membership. Macedonia is trying to reach the ethics-in-government standards that the EU requires before it applies and Ukraine's 45 million people wait eagerly in the wings. This politically unstable state looks like it'll be put on the back burner along with Turkey.

"If Irish voters torpedo the Lisbon Treaty in a second referendum in October there will be no further enlargement of the Union. Even Croatia may find the EU door bolted shut." This is *Irish Times* European Editor Jamie Smyth's interpretation of the current thinking of the German government.[93]

TL: the crash diet article - no consumption of any new countries, no matter how light, like Croatia.

---

93   Jamie Smyth, *The Irish Times*, 5 May 2009

77 Avoid a protest vote: punish Fianna Fáil later.

The electoral knives are out and justifiably so for Fianna Fáil. There's one good reason *100 Reasons* has decided to leave it until now to quote Brian Cowen.

Now by God, he's ready. 'I have read the Treaty since I was last asked that question.'

"But there is one thing for sure, that if Ireland is to prosper, Ireland must be an integral part of that organisation and that our destiny is totally and utterly linked up with that – not only as a marketplace, but in terms of investment strategy, which has brought so much investment: five times more to Ireland than any other OECD country of foreign direct investment. That has provided us with many of the jobs and you with many of the sub-supply opportunities into those sectors, that has provided us [with] unprecedented employment growth over the past ten years."[94]

He's right, but he's been wrong about so much that it's difficult to see what use the main Government party will be in this debate. Throughout the first one, Cowen refused to consult or co-operate with his Opposition colleagues. Entertainingly, Libertas still used a poster showing the three party leaders Cowen, Kenny and Gilmore all together in one shot sharing a joke, like they've just walked home from a party together. That was a coup, as those smiles must've happened only once for about half-a-second. A photographic misnomer. Cowen com-

---

94   Brian Cowen's speech to the Dublin Chamber, Fri 6 Feb 2009

mented at one stage that he didn't think Fine Gael were pulling their weight on the Yes Campaign. Kenny was livid and Gilmore commented "I think there are occasions, in the country's interest, where the Taoiseach will have to resist the temptation of giving the Opposition parties a kick every time he sees us." The Taoiseach has been arrogant, defensive and dogmatic ever since and will be punished by the electorate in the next general election more than he was in the local and European contests. His communication with the Opposition has gotten worse with little or no consultation going on between them over the Banking bail-out and the provisions of the Budget or the subsequent mini-Budget.

Only belatedly did Fianna Fáil enact a cursory consultation with opposition colleagues about the text for the legal guarantees or the enabling legislation. After much radio silence, Dick Roche finally announced in May that the referendum would be in the autumn and in July, the date was released. What a surprise. This go-it-alone strategy has not been helpful. Last year, our benighted leader needlessly got himself stick in a rut of perceived ignorance when he admitted not to have actually read the whole Treaty. Now by God, he's ready. "I have read the Treaty since I was last asked that question."[95]

The Government have also disbanded the National Forum on Europe, the independent body made up of elected representatives from all parties which heard submssions from all sections of society and travelled around the country in an information drive. The forum may not have been publicised as well as it could have been, but judging by the plenary debates it held and the quality and lucidity of its publications in terms of the Summary Guide to the Treaty and Chairman Maurice Hayes' reports, it seemed rash, bordering on self-destructive for the

95   *Irish Independent*, 23 June 2009

Government to disband it before the question of the Lisbon Treaty had finally been put to bed.

This Government and high-handedness go together like a horse and carriage moving forward shoulder-to-shoulder tripping arse-over-tit frothing foot-in-mouth indignation over bare-chested jiggly man-boob portraits, so to speak, in a political sense.

It's important to separate the issue of dissatisfaction with the Government and the vote on Lisbon. Justified anger over where the axe will fall heaviest as per Colm McCarthy's cuts recommendations has nothing to do with the Treaty. And arrogance and complacency, of course, are not confined to the Soldiers of Destiny. It was interesting to gauge in the research of this book, the levels of co-operation from and access granted to the main parties who advocate a Yes to Lisbon. There's a reason apart from, say, political bias, why Labour representatives are more heavily quoted than Fine Gael and the Greens. Michéal Martin and Dick Roche make as formidable, committed and approachable a team as their Labour counterparts in securing a Yes vote, but *100 Reasons* is nonetheless looking forward to kicking their party to the kerb in the next elections.

TL: Bertie's signature, that's it.

78 "Sabotaging the work of twenty-seven Governments over seven years."

That's how the grand old man of Irish politics Dr. Garret Fitzgerald described a No vote to Lisbon. He went on to state "there is nothing to fear in this Treaty."[96]

To remind you why you might come to respect this opinion, *100 Reasons* would like to briefly outline why Garret is one of the most qualified politicians the country has ever produced.

Dr. Garret Fitzgerald may not ever have been able to get a handle on his crazy hair, learned to wear matching socks or give a damn for the simple soundbite when a rapid-fire and long-winded dissection of the issue at stake would do better, but he always knew what he was talking about.

In his political heyday as Minister for Foreign Affairs, his ten-year reign as leader of Fine Gael or as twice-elected Taoiseach in the 1980s, Garret earned great respect from his colleagues both in his own party and outside it. In these dark days, economic expertise is so desperately required on Government front benches that RTE Economics editor George Lee felt it his duty to chuck in the dayjob and try to save the country. In those dark days, Garret was an economist who lectured in political economy in UCD for fourteen years and went into politics after he was well established in his subject. He was also a barrister, but sure never mind that, he slotted in the King's Inn's exams on a wet week when he was at a loose end. He was a correspondent on economic affairs for the BBC, *The Finan-*

96 *The Irish Times* 10 June 2008

cial Times and *The Economist* and he was Managing Director of the Economist Intelligence Unit of Ireland from 1961-67.

Garret is acknowledged to have been one of Ireland's most masterful Ministers for Foreign Affairs who expertly guided us through the waters of joining the EEC in 1973 and in this capacity, he presided over the Council of Ministers from January to June 1975. This constant gaze beyond the national scene throughout his career gives Garret's view on the future direction of the EU much gravitas. At 83, he's mentally on-the-ball enough to continue delivering terrific weekly columns to the *Irish Times*.

> ## Fitzgerald has described opponents of the Lisbon Treaty as 'nitpickers of the extreme right and left.'

So have we established that Garret, a man of great ability and achievement knows a little bit about Ireland, economics and Europe (and therefore neutrality, tax and institutional pitfalls)?

Fitzgerald has described opponents of the Lisbon Treaty as 'nitpickers of the extreme right and left.' He reminded the electorate of the Irish influence in the drawing up of the Treaty, saying 'it was our Treaty more than anyone else's.'

TL: the man practically invented the EU, it was his fevered dream.

79 It's essential for our economy.

Membership of the EU has been the cornerstone of our economic success.

Ireland has been able to capitalise on its enviable position geographically, linguistically and monetarily as the only English-speaking member of the Eurozone with a highly trained, educated workforce positioned on the edge of a single European market of 500 million people.

Membership of the EU has been central to Ireland's economic development. It is the fundamental basis for Ireland's remarkable economic success since the early 1990s.

The investment by the then EEC in infrastructure and training that started in 1973 started to bear fruit by the 1990s in tandem with the economic policies of our governments. We were able to attract five times more foreign direct investment than any other OECD country. In 2006, investment by US companies in Ireland (€83 billion) exceeded combined US investment in China, India, Russia and Brazil (€73 billion). 960 foreign firms employing 138,000 people have set up in Ireland. OK, granted half of them seem to be winding things up as fast as they can nowadays and moving to Poland – not only taking our jobs, but our Polish girlfriends with them – but without being a respected, influential Member State of the EU we've no hope of persuading multinationals to stick it out in Ireland through the recession. One million jobs have been created here since 1973.[97]

When we joined in 1973, our GDP per capita was 58 per cent of the European average and by the end of 2007, Irish GDP per

97   IBEC

capita had reached 144 per cent of the EU average. The year 1973 is special for Irish businessman Martin Naughton, who started Glen Dimplex then. He said "I have seen at first hand the extraordinary impact it had on my business and this country." He's done pretty well, Naughton, that self-made Louth multimillionaire and the great thing is, you won't hear a bad word said about him, at least not round de to-w-nnn (elongate those vowels), hey.

Only 18 per cent of our exports now go to the UK, compared with 45 per cent which go to the European Union. Ireland's membership of the EU and participation in the Single European Market has been the most significant factor in ending our country's economic dependence on the United Kingdom.[98]

TL: the 'all boats rise with the tide' idea applies better to countries sometimes than to people.

---

98   Sub-Ctte Report on Ireland's Future in the EU, Nov. 2008

80 Improved democratic representation

Citizens are directly represented at Union level in the European Parliament.

Member States are represented in the European Council by their Heads of State and Government and by their Government in the Council of Ministers, themselves democratically responsible either to their National Parliaments or their citizens.

Article 10 of the TEU is like a Venn Diagram of democracy. Shall we draw one? We're aware that other books about politics have tables and diagrams, so we want some. We're nearly at the end of the list and *100 Reasons* hasn't had a diagram. It's the right time to slot one in, definitely.

See Venn Diagram below:

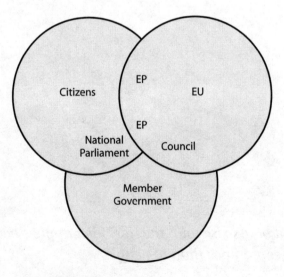

TL: Article 8A [10] TEU

81 Give Silvio a break.

Silvio Berlusconi needs a little lift now his wife is going to make the McCartney-Mills divorce look like an amicable post-nuptial settlement.

You've got to hand it to Silvio, while we've been busy trying to improve the looks of the Irish populace, he was on a selfless pre-election drive to improve the looks of the European Parliament. The 72-year-old was tireless in his recruitment and re-packaging of actresses, Miss World models, TV presenters and *Big Brother* contestants as candidates for the European election. It didn't really fly for Silvio, but you can't fault him for effort.

His wife Veronica, 52, a former actress herself and very pretty lady views this great work for the Euro-good, as the pathetic pawings and canoodlings of an aging lothario. She's had it and has kicked him out. Maybe she's right, maybe Berlusconi had other motives for his thwarted attempt to deploy his Euro-babes to last June's elections. Maybe it was to distract the Commission with cleavage, legs and big hair from giving him any more grief over immigration policy, the rescue of Italian airline Al-Italia and the problem of waste disposal in Naples. Silvio may bristle at EU interference in his demesne, but he wants Lisbon to go through, so that he can be viewed as a great European.

After the lower house Italian parliament unanimously approved the Treaty for ratification, Berlusconi expressed satisfaction, calling it "a particularly important result because the whole of parliament and the government united to support an ambitious project." On the question of Ireland's rejection, he said "From our part, we will indicate for the approval of the European Union's treaty by all the remaining twenty-six member states, besides Ireland." He left it on an ominous note "The 27th, Ireland, will have to present its own solution."[99] 'You broke it, you fix it', that's his take. When it comes to his marriage, his wife's take is 'you broke it, it's broken, now fuck off.'

> ...subsequent divorce proceedings do point to old Silvio being a hard dog to keep on the porch...

Right now, Berlusconi's pretending that his wandering eyes, hands and whatever else has nothing to do with the matter, but complains about opposition parties putting his wife up to the divorce. "I am indignant," Berlusconi said. "Veronica has fallen into a trap. And I know who she is being advised by. Or rather, being incited by."[100] It apparently has nothing to do with his attendance at the birthday party for an 18-year-old aspirant model who calls him 'Daddy.' Nice. The billionaire media magnate has accused the rival publications and TV stations of 'media criminality', so perhaps there's been a bit of misrepresentation here, but the separation and subsequent divorce proceedings do point to old Silvio being a hard dog to keep on the porch, as the American phrase puts it. A Bari-based investigation dug up allegations of lovely ladies being paid to entertain old Silvio, but he maintains he's never paid for sex, as "I never understood what the satisfaction is when you are missing the pleasure of conquest."[101] You see, he's an old fashioned gentleman-cad after all.

His wronged missus Veronica tends to write to the newspapers or hold a press conference when she's pissed off at him, rather than send him a nasty text or let the cat pee on his Armani

---

99   www.topnewsin.com, 19 June 2008
100   *The Guardian*, 4 May 2009
101   *The Guardian* 24 June 2009

suits. Suffice to say, it was never the healthiest of marriages. So go on, give Silvio a wee sliver of respite. Times are tough – his hair plugs haven't really taken, his teenage pals make all kinds of cultural references he doesn't get, he's getting gip from the Commission, the G8 summit at recent earthquake-hit L'Aquila was viewed an organisational shambles and he's worried about how much of his reputed €4.5 billion fortune will go to his ex-wife. So go on, give poor Silvio a break.

TL: Silvio's John Thomas, I mean John Hancock, I mean, you know what I mean.

82 Lisbon will improve R&D in European economies.

Projects like the EU's Seventh Framework Programme (FP7) investing in trans-European research projects are a way out of this financial black hole.

Being part of the EU opened up a vast market to our hi-tech goods and services industries to export to and encouraged foreign companies to invest here. As Ireland has progressively become less and less competitive at attracting foreign investment since 2000, developing Ireland's knowledge economy is the smart way forward. The Seventh Framework Programme aims to provide €50 billion for scientific research between 2007 and 2013.

It represents great opportunities for Ireland's academic researchers, small-to-medium businesses, multinationals and health professionals to take part in trans-European R&D projects forging business and academic links with their counterparts across the continent.

With FP7 funding, IBM Ireland participated in an innovative project aimed at enabling desktop computers to employ cognitive reasoning more like human beings by structuring information in a way close to that in the human brain. It must've been difficult to mimic our 'oh-look-a-bird' human mental flightiness. Ta-daaa! IBM is proud to unveil the computer of tomorrow: TOMMO's artificial intelligence is geared towards random reasoning factoring in ignorance, prejudice and jealousy, when not daydreaming about sex, power and snacks every 30-40 seconds.

IBM Ireland received funding of some €745,000 for that project, which it ran in collaboration with fifteen European partners. Senior Manager Marie Wallace said "There is the financial support, which is very attractive; the network connections to researchers across Europe, and the opportunity to carry out applied research, with a three-to-five year application." She didn't mention when TOMMO's vast intellect would be available at reasonable cost to the public. In the meantime, your little brother will do the job just fine.

It's not just in information & communications technology that FP7 is the main funding instrument for collaborative research, but also in agriculture, fisheries, health, sustainable energy, environment, transport, security, socio-economic sciences and the humanities.

The National Director of FP7, Dr Imelda Lambkin of Enterprise Ireland, says it "is the single biggest source of funding available locally to Irish researchers." But she would say that, wouldn't she? Well as it happens, it's true. When national funding is plummeting under pressure from the Government to make cuts across the board, this EU budget is steady and locked-in across the six years. Under Lambkin, there are 34 National Contact Points (NCPs) or experts in their field from whom to access information as to what projects would suit particular applicants.

Ireland benefited from the previous FP6 programme (2002-2006) to the tune of €200 million and intends to squeeze €600 million out of FP7.[102] That's the plan.

TL: OK, OK, fine, there's no mention of FP7 in Lisbon, but without Lisbon, we can kiss FP8 through FP327 a sweet goodbye.

---

102   Enterprise Ireland.

83 Protects children's rights

Children's Rights will be embedded into the fundamental legal texts of the EU for the first time.

The European Children's Network (EURONET) represents children's rights NGOs across Europe. EURONET have campaigned for the inclusion of children's rights in the European Treaties since 1995 and have contributed extensively to the inclusion of a reference to children's rights in the Treaties.

The thing about children is that they're so disorganised. Ask them to prepare a policy document for you and they're forever procrastinating...

Now EURONET isn't much of an acronym, is it? These groups are supposed to at least remind you or hint darkly at what they might be up to – EURATOM does Atomic energy. You see, it's in the title. Where are the children at? Instead of EUROKID or EUROCHIL or EUMINOR, they decided to forget about children entirely.

Anyway, sorry about that – EURONET welcomed this children's rights section in Article 3 of the Treaty. Now promoting children's rights is folded into all of the EU's internal and external objectives.

The Union... shall promote... protection of the rights of the child.

In its relations with the wider world, the Union shall contribute to... eradication of poverty and the protection of human rights, in particular the rights of the child... as well as the strict observance and the development of international law...

This will mean the the EU will be able to safeguard children's rights in all policy areas like consumer protection rights, asylum rights and trade policy.

Fergus Finlay, Chief Executive of Barnardos in Ireland, told *100 Reasons* "everything that puts the rights and needs of children more to the top of the agenda is very positive for children and families particularly in a climate where despite all the rhetoric, support for children and families is actually declining. I think it's a very positive message."

These reforms unfortunately allow children's voices to be heard and everyone with any sense knows that children should be seen and not heard. So maybe this provision protecting children's rights won't safeguard adults' rights to enjoy a bit of fucking peace and quiet to sit for five minutes, FIVE MINUTES, that's all we ask, to do the fucking SUDOKU.

Also don't forget that children can use the citizen's initiative. All they need to do is get a million of their friends (the ones old enough to write) to sign a petition to table a proposal to the Commission. The thing about children is that they're so disorganised. Ask them to prepare a policy document for you and they're forever procrastinating with frogspawn experiments, colouring books, army manoeuvres and dressing-up sessions. In short, children are inherently unserious about defending their rights in an organised way. They expect us to do it for them. The lazy little gits.

TL: Article 2 [3] TEU

84 Eurovision survives

Calm down now – there's nothing in Lisbon that harms the status of the Eurovision Song Contest.

Eurovision is safe, unless we send another fucking puppet.

Eurovision is the only realm of European achievement in which Ireland reigns supreme with a record seven wins, although with our last glorious victory back in 1996, we'd need to get our act together fairly soon now.

Nothing in the Lisbon Treaty threatens that inexpensive to watch, yet prohibitive to mount, high entertainment night-in for teenage girls, gay men, women under 40, people who pretend to only find it enjoyable when viewed through a thick screen of irony and well, we suppose, people who just really, really love it, like...

Past double-champion Johnny Logan, who merits mentioning as he had the good grace to take the piss out of himself by returning to his 'Hold Me Now' moment of triumph and the bad grace to do it as part of a McDonalds 'Eurosaver' meal ad. In the absence of an Irish Tarantino resurrecting him Travolta-like for a gritty turn as a force of sweaty malevolence, it's as much of a comeback as the gold laméd smoothie will make.

Ex-MEP Patricia McKenna, no, no, we mean Dana, aka the former-MEP-formerly-known-as-Dana, Rosemary Scallan, we always mix those two up. The first Irish winner of Eurovision beat that leathery lothario Julio Iglesias with her Derry innocence and moral universe that would've made Dev proud to have her succeed him – with some intervening years of course – as President, but alas, it wasn't to be. *100 Reasons* is reliably informed he watched the contest with rapt attention while slurping vegetable soup in the Áras in March 1970. Then to add insult to Dana's legacy, our musical Europeers voted a scary musclebound[103] Israeli called Dana International to the top spot in 1998.

Terry Wogan. Come back Terry, we miss that that offscreen eyebrow raise – the Eurovision's camp enough without Graham Norton's double entendres...

Eurovision is safe, unless we send another fucking puppet.

TL: The Death Metal Disco Lordi Clause, which doesn't have a number, but is written in sanskrit backwards in invisible ink underneath Article 66, subsection 5.9 TEU

---

103   Because she used to be a he, in a further dig at original Dana's B&W view
of the world. The hairy fake-tanned bare-arsed cheek of it all.

85 Helps the EU stand up to the US

An EU with a more coherent foreign policy and smoother voting arrangements would prove a challenge to Uncle Sam's self-imposed role as world bul-we mean-policeman, yes that's it, policeman. Even though a new dawn is here with Barack in the House, the US is still the muscle-bound teenager kicking sand in people's eyes.

> Soft power might just be a silly buzz phrase, but it sure beats nuclear arsenal or dirty bomb as a deterrent concept.

The EU's status as a global actor which could speak with one voice would be vastly improved with Lisbon giving us our double-jobbing High Rep and voting arrangements that encourage consensus and agreement over common foreign policy.

For seventeen years in a row, the UN General Assembly voted against the US's trade blockade of Cuba. In 2008, it was 185 Member States against three – the US, Israel and Pilau – while the Marshall islands and Micronesia abstained (so that international browbeating really seems to have worked). It took until Obama became President for the policy to start to be dismantled. However if the US were up to bullyboy tactics elsewhere, it would not be deterred by the various military capabilities of the EU Member States, but it would think twice about the economic implications of a possible trade blockade.

It would have to be an extreme circumstance for all the Member States to reach the consensus to temporarily pull the plug on trade with the States, but millions marching in anti-war demonstrations and UN declarations against the current oil wars weren't much of a damper.

BUT if in 2050, worse neo-con Republicans than Bush & Cheney are on the brink of going to war with China in Africa over who controlled natural resources there, it would be a good card to carry, because if we ever see that war, al-Qaeda will seem like a quaint anachronism of a more innocent age (and then the only one worth carrying will be your organ donor card.)

Soft power might just be a silly buzz phrase, but it sure beats nuclear arsenal or dirty bomb as a deterrent concept.

TL: no mention of anti-US trade blockades or war with China on African soil in the Treaties.

86 Abolishes the current EU structure of three policy area pillars

Now if these pillars that were established in 1993 after Maastricht are abolished, or as it could be visualised, demolished (is there a need for a diagram here!?) like Nelson's column – it's a good job this isn't an audio book or we'd have to engage in a full-power digression on the EU-wide pronunciation of column like the nice manly, Irish Christian name, Colm and NOT with a hulking, great, dirty, big, 'U' spoken, out-loud, by accountancy teachers from Laois – think about how many times a day an account-ancy teacher has to say the word!

> The Treaty would bulldoze the pillars and they'd all fall down higgledy-piggledy and be no more...

Yes, a lot, so the former is the correct and most aesthetically pleasing verbal treatment of the other word for 'pillar', glad that's settled – what's the point now in telling you about them? [the pillars are still free-standing structures – no abolishment/demolishment has, as yet, occurred – editor]. Ah yes-

The first pillar covers economic and social policy and is based around the establishment of the European Community, including the Single Market. This centred around the three communities of the EC, the European Community for Atomic Energy (EURATOM) and the former European Coal and Steel Community (ECSC), which ceased to exist in 2002.

The second pillar deals with the Common Foreign and Security Policy and the third deals with Justice and Home Affairs. There are two strands of this third pillar, one dealing with cross-border issues like immigration and asylum and the other based around Police and Judicial Co-operation in criminal matters. (Picture a gaggle of cops and judges chasing a gang of hardened Westies shinning up the Millenium Spire by giving each other boosts and you're there – you're full-square *in* the issue, *on* the Euro-wavelength).

The Treaty would bulldoze the pillars and they'd all fall down higgledy-piggledy and be no more, thus erasing an intergovernmental system and moving all policy towards majority voting while retaining special voting procedures (unanimity) for the Common Foreign and Security Policy. Immigration, asylum, police and judicial co-operation will thus no longer have a separate pillar, but Ireland, with the UK, will have an opt-out/opt-in with regard to these areas. Fifteen legal instruments spread across the three pillars are reduced to the number of five contained in Article 249 of the TFEU. It's supposed to make it all simpler and more efficient. So there.

TL: 249 [289-292] TFEU

87 Lisbon reinforces the legitimacy of the UN.

Declaration 13 recognises the primacy of the UN for the maintenance of international peace and security.

This is a nice reminder that the Lisbon reforms bringing in a High Rep to coordinate external policy does not envisage the EU in any role of world policeman.

100 Reasons asked MEP Proinsias de Rossa if this assuaged fears of this happening. "I welcome the provision. However I do not harbour such fears. I am fully aware of the limits to the role the EU can play in international affairs. In some respects this is a great pity, as for instance in the Middle East, where a more pro-active political role would be of benefit to world peace."

> Declaration 13 recognises the primacy of the UN for the maintenance of international peace and security.

That's the UN's job and the UN is given more legitimacy by this declaration being set down. After the mess of the US threatening to ignore UN declarations, it's much needed.

This is the declaration that guarantees that the provisions governing the Common Security and Defence Policy *do not prejudice the specific character of the security and defence policy of the Member States.*

UN Secretary General Ban Ki Moon said during a speech in July at Dublin Castle "Let me assure you that Ireland's participation in EU military and civilian missions is fully compatible with its traditional support of the United Nations. This is not a zero-sum game in which more support for one institution means less for the other. We are in this together."[104] The wee dote had a phonetic pronunciation at the speech's end to make sure he nailed his audience: the words were 'Shaymus Heeney.' Even though he made reference to our limit this year on the extent of overseas aid – his message was clear – Ireland is a valued member of the UN that has contributed much; at the same time, the UN and the EU espoused the same values. Join the dots.

TL: Declaration 13, not exactly in the Treaty, but just over to the left of it – there it is, between the biro and the coffee cup.

---

104   Footnote IIEA, 7 July, 2009

88 Better organised crime prevention

Lisbon will allow for stronger legislation to combat cross-border crime like human trafficking and sexual exploitation of women and children.

Lisbon changes the decision-making process in the area of freedom, security and justice, including crimes in relation to trafficking in persons – in particular, women and children, (Article 69b) and sexual exploitation of women and children (Article 69f).

In the past ten years, over half-a-million women have been trafficked into Europe and in a one-year period from 2007 to 2008, €50 billion worth of drugs and guns were smuggled into Europe by criminal gangs.[105]

The EU's strategy to counter trafficking is to promote and protect human rights and act against discrimination, placing the victims at the heart of EU legislation. This is in recognition of the fact that minorities, indigenous people, women and children are particularly vulnerable. Even though the world in all its good and bad has come to Ireland since the 1990s, it's still shocking to us that there are trafficked women (and children) working here in the sex trade against their will and imprisoned in apartments around the country.

The EU employ a broad gamut of approaches including law enforcement, police administration, anti-criminal border controls, victim support, prevention and the aforementioned action

---

105   ec.europa.eu

against discrimination. The aim of this new legislation is to forge better links, communication and co-operation between police forces, customs and the specialist agencies of men in dark glasses and suits. The Treaty doesn't give Europol carte blanche to take over murder investigations in Carlow, as they must have agreement from local police.

...from 2007 to 2008, €50 billion worth of drugs and guns were smuggled into Europe by criminal gangs.

The application of coercive measures shall be the exclusive responsibility of the the competent national authorities.

With this, *100 Reasons* pressed delete on all our 'loose cannon/maverick Düsseldorf cop at war with Limerick gangs' script noodlings.

TL: Article 69 [87] TFEU

89 It'll help EU Members combat domestic violence.

In its general efforts to eliminate inequalities between women and men, the Union will aim in its different policies to combat all kinds of domestic violence. The Member States should take all necessary measures to prevent and punish these criminal acts and to support and protect the victims.

Prior to this, the EU had issued guidelines as to how best to approach domestic violence based on multilateral agreements with other nation groups. Now it's a declaration. The tenets were based around

> The problem with domestic violence is that it's hard to get accurate information on its prevalence...

the UN Secretary-General's in-depth study on all forms of violence against women (2006), resulting in UN resolutions like 61/143 on intensification of efforts to eliminate all forms of violence against women and the work on indicators on violence carried out by Ms Yakin Ertük, UN Special Rapporteur on Violence against Women (2008.)

The guidelines define "the term 'violence against women' means any act of gender-based violence that results in, or is likely to result in, physical, sexual or psychological harm or suffering to women, including threats of such acts, coercion or arbitrary deprivation of liberty, whether occurring in public or in private life".

The problem with domestic violence is that it's hard to get

accurate information on its prevalence, although local communities will already be aware of who suffers from it. It is only when the victims themselves feel that safeguards will be put in place to help them once they report the abuse, will they come forward. In some Member countries, for such safety to come into being, societal attitudes to women and violence towards them must change.

The first strand of the EU's policy against it is to rule against any legislation that is discrimatory towards women and girls and then to promote anti-discrimination information campaigns. The second is to increase the quality of information on the incidents of domestic abuse, so that strategies tailored to each region can be initiated. Thirdly, the States must ensure that perpetrators of violence against women must be punished before the courts. This entails the training of police and law enforcement officers and legal aid lawyers as to how to deal impartially with the victims.

All conditions that encourage victims to testify are being considered: from proper protection of them and witnesses to the creation of funds whereby the victims are no longer economically dependent on the perpetrators of violence. In Ireland, the EU DAPHNE programme has supported activities and research by the Immigrant Council, the Rape Crisis Centre and COSC the National Office for the Prevention of Domestic, Sexual and Gender-based Violence. Wasn't Daphne the glamorous one in Scooby Doo's gang? Another strangely apposite acronym from the EU backroom squirrels...

The victims of domestic violence directly and indirectly can be kids, so it is very positive for the rights of children too.

TL: Declaration to promote the fight against domestic violence Declaration on Article III-116.

90 Cheaper air travel

Cheap flights are as much thanks to EU Air Liberalisation policies as they are to Michael 'fuck you and your mother too' O'Leary.

Before the the single market for air travel, the aviation industry used to be highly regulated and ruled by national flag carrying state-owned airlines. In a three-stage air liberalisation strategy over a decade from 1987, all commercial restrictions were removed, like what routes an airline could fly, the setting of fares and the number of flights. All EU airlines have the freedom of cabotage, which is the right to operate services on any route within the EU. The single air transport market was extended to include Iceland, Norway and Switzerland. Increased competition has driven prices down and brought increased choice for consumers. Between 1992 and 2006, the number of routes with more than two competitors rose by 300 per cent.[106] The Commission is hammering out a Common Aviation Area deal with Euromed countries and neighbouring countries to the east to extend them the same market freedoms.

International aviation is much more regulated as it's based on bilateral agreements between countries restricting the number of airlines, routes, flight numbers and given destinations. The EU is working to extend its aviation policy to make any such bilateral agreements be in line with the freedom of operation in the internal market and make sure all EU airlines have equality of access to international routes. In 2002, the ECJ ruled that eight of these bilateral agreements with the US were contrary to the EU Treaties. The EU has attempted to modify these agreements in what's known as the Open Skies Treaty with the US.

---

106   ec.europa.eu Flying Together 2007 doc

The European Aviation Safety Agency (EASA) was established in 2002 to work in tandem with the National Aviation agencies. Post 9/11, it harmonised security measures at all EU airports. This is put into place so that you can get aggravated to precisely the same degree all over Europe from Beauvais to Schipol.

> Business culture comes from the top and if an ethos could be said to permeate the company, it would be cheerful callousness.

In 2005, the EU brought in new regulations on compensation and assistance for passengers in the case of denied boarding, cancellations, overbooking and long flight delays. Passengers denied seats due to overbooking are entitled to €250 compensation for short-haul flights and up to €600 for long-haul flights. Airlines, especially the no-frills carriers, accepted these new rules under duress. Any weapons EU consumers have in seeking redress against low service culture airlines for lack of customer support are vital. Ryanair treats its staff so poorly in terms of pay and conditions that you expect surliness at every turn and are thus pleasantly surprised at their general professionalism as they chirpily impose the rapacious baggage weight add-on fees and offer prohibitively priced in-flight snacks. Business culture comes from the top and if an ethos could be said to permeate the company, it would be cheerful callousness.

O'Leary's been griping that the Commission isn't cracking down on airlines like Air France, Al-Italia and British Airways who are being propped up by their governments. The Commission had blocked Ryanair's takeover of Aer Lingus, believing it would lead to higher prices once the airline's main Irish rival has been vanquished. O'Leary has on a number of occasions accused Brussels of bias against his company.Yet Michael O'Leary supports a Yes vote for the second referendum. He knows which wing Ryanair's bread is buttered on and has said the company would not exist were if not for the EU. "We will campaign for a Yes and we hope to be Europe's biggest airline in the next few years," he said. In typical forthright terms, he urged voters ignore some of the 'lunatic fringe' of the No Campaign especially "that bunch of economic illiterates, Sinn Féin, that is urging a No vote and I would urge that we should do the exact opposite."[107] There are many things you could accuse O'Leary of, but being a poor businessman is not one of them.

TL: We hate it when he's right...

---

107   *Irish Examiner*, 18 Dec, 2008

91 Because Ulick says nyet!

In keeping with the aviation theme, Mayo businessman Ulick McEvady weighed in on the No side of the campaign last year. McEvaddy is the CEO of Omega Air (set up 20 years ago with his brother Des) that supplies the US with in-flight refuelling services and cargo planes, specialising in the carthorses of the industry, Boeing 707s. Ulick is ex-Irish army, where he spent 10 years, first as a transport captain and then as a military intelligence officer. In Ireland? Really? Does that count? Apparently it does. This background has stood him in good stead in dealing with the Yanks with hairy nostrils and stripes on their shoulderpads. He spent time on the Russian desk and he is fluent, which is however only useful when dealing with the Russian military, not the US, just the Russians.

Ulick is a political animal familiar with the Dáil visitors bar and despite friendships with Charlie McCreevy and Mary Harney, he's a traditional Fine Gael voter and benefactor. A 'No' vote must be very important to him, if he is willing to publicly campaign against the party he traditionally enabled, his friends in Fianna Fáil and all his fellow captains of Irish industry. We can't claim Ulick's not politically engaged. After all, he's read the Treaty 4 times coming to the conclusion that it's 'unintelligible drivel.'[108] *100 Reasons* wonders on which reading did this dawn on him...

McEvaddy kept a low profile prior to stepping in to campaign publicly for a No vote last year and has only popped up in media reports occasionally, once through his friendship with the Minister for Health, when she got in hot water for staying at his South of France villa free of charge. It'd be a bit rich for a multi-

---

108   *The Irish Times*, 23 August 2008

millionaire to charge his mates to stay in his holiday home though, wouldn't it? He was appointed to the board of Knock airport and lobbied for it to open up to US military flights, but this proposal was rejected by the other board members who included the Archbishop of Tuam thus ruling out the entertaining prospect of the Virgin Mary, St. Joseph and St. John the Evangelist appearing to (or on, or maybe perhaps flying alongside) planeloads of terrified 18-year-old grunts from Iowa. After an eighteen-year absence, McEvaddy was re-appointed to the Knock board in 2007. When asked in that year about the possibility of there ever being military flights coming into Knock he said "Never say never, I have huge connections with the US military and if it came to using them, I would."[109]

He's read the Treaty 4 times coming to the conclusion that it's 'unintelligible drivel.'

In March 2007, Omega were awarded a $24 million contract to provide inflight refuelling to the US Navy, a contract renewed a year later adding a further $30 million to the deal.[110] Omega Air has long since specialised in work with US air giant Boeing, which is constantly vying with its European competitor Airbus in a race of two. Omega became the world's leading authority on replacing the old, noisy engines on 707s with a Pratt & Whitney system which saves fuel and brings them into line with modern international standards, whereas the Europeans were trying to establish Airbus's quieter engine as the international standard.[111]

'4-Times' McEvaddy climbed on the No campaign bandwagon quite literally, with a speech outside the Libertas campaign bus

---

109   *The Irish Times*, 22 January 2007
110   US Dept. Of Defense, Security & Co-operation Agency Press Release, 19 March 2007
111   Sam Smyth, *Irish Independent*, 28 Aug 1999

sporting a large font 'Don't let Brussels set our taxes' printed along the side. It was a good photo opportunity on Merrion Square in April 2008 for the two businessmen to shoot the breeze. McEvaddy and Ganley have so much in common, their friends must've been trying to introduce them for years. Both are highly successful entrepreneurs, both run businesses supplying equipment and services to the US military and both really, really dislike the Lisbon Treaty. They can probably finish each other's sentences.

It'll be interesting to see whether McEvaddy again adopts a public role for 'Lisbon 2: Last Chance'.

TL: I-lick, U-lick, everybody licks the highly combustible and not very tasty colour-coded aviation fuel... yuch, Shell: always leaves a nasty aftertaste.

92 It will help eliminate corruption in Ireland.

Archbishop Martin reminds us that few people would say that the malpractice which is at the root of the economic crisis was Brussels-driven, rather than home-grown. "It is useful to remind ourselves that there are very few who would say that the malpractice which is at the root of much of the current economic crisis was Brussels driven, rather than home-grown. In many ways, Brussels is not the problem, but it is recognised more and more as an essential part of the solution."[112]

If Archbishop Martin had been giving the sermons round our way, maybe *100 Reasons* would still be attending Mass. Decent oratory occurs in the church almost as seldom as in Dáil Eireann. Either that or maybe, like *100 Reasons*, the Archbishop's favourite action film is *Die Hard:*[113]

Deputy Chief Robinson: You listen to me you little asshole! **McClane**: Asshole? I'm not the one who just got butt-fucked on national TV, *Dwayne*! Now, you listen to me, jerk-off, if you're not a part of the solution, you're a part of the problem. Quit being a part of the fucking problem and put the other guy back on!

So there you have it - conclusive evidence that the Archbishop thinks of Brian Cowen as Dwayne T. Robinson *and* every so often, Archbishop Martin cracks open a cold one and kicks back with the Bruce-meister for some explosions and cracking of wise...

---

112   Archbishop Diarmuid Martin, IIEA, 3 March 2009
113   It's the bit after the LAPD's RV has just been bazookaed to kingdom come and McClane is getting a lecture on the walkie from the dumb-dumb Deputy chief.

He – the Archbishop, not Bruce, he's a Republican – said also at a meeting with the Commission President in May that "Ireland needs Europe, but Europe also needs Ireland." *100 Reasons* wishes it could share his optimism. But then again, our only faith lies in a Yes vote, not in God Almighty, our Lord and Saviour. It's a shame really, as it's a good argument to have God on your side.

Quit being a part of the fucking problem and put the other guy back on!

TL: Not there, just conjecture from about the only Church leader who has any moral authority left.

93 Biffo came back from Brussels with the protocol bacon.

All the legal guarantees on issues of concern for the Irish electorate have been secured and made legally ironclad by the commitment from all Member States to attach them as a protocol to the next accession Treaty.

"We came here with two aims. Ireland wanted firm legal guarantees. We got them. We wanted a commitment to a protocol. We got that."[114] Our beleaguered Taoiseach knew that he couldn't come back with anything less than protocol status for the guarantees and it looked for a while that Gordon Brown was going to be the sticking block against the achievement of this goal. The last thing Brown wanted was to re-open the Lisbon debate in the current UK political scene where he's on the backfoot so much it's a miracle he's able to walk at all. The genius move of annexing the guarantees onto the next accession Treaty, which will probably be Croatia in 2010 or 2011, allowed agreement that there would be no need to re-ratify the Treaty in domestic parliaments across the continent. The states that had been opposed to the guarantees being given protocol status like Poland, the Netherlands and Slovenia were thus won around once they knew that they wouldn't have to re-negotiate the Treaty itself again as the guarantees' *content is fully compatible with the Treaty.*

Shock horror, the guarantees are expressed in simple, lucid English like *Nothing in the Treaty of Lisbon makes any change of any kind, for any member state, to the extent or operation of the competence of the European Union in rela-*

114   *The Irish Times* 20 June 2009

tion to taxation. Clear, as like, crystal, not muddy crystal, but gleaming, transparent, super-shiney prose any self-respecting 11-year-old (budding politician) could grasp.

Despite the fact that the guarantees cover each main red herring of the No Campaign last time, apparently we weren't listening and it wasn't these issues which were of concern at all, it was completely different ones entirely. It's

> the tenor of the debate will be petulant, the information deliberately misleading and the atmosphere increasingly belligerent. Should be fun.

that old 'move-the-goalposts' type of argument that men and women have all the time, just when you think you're calmly debating one thing, apparently it's now all about that BBQ when you spent too much time chatting to Sean's missus, who just happens to be electric blue of eye and blond of hue and hot of curve. Mary Lou now says "The treaty does not protect workers' rights, itdoes not protect the delivery of public services, and it is the next stepping stone towards the centralisation of European power." But, wait a second, why no mention of abortion, neutrality or tax, Mary? Because these guarantees have taken them off the table as factors? Hmmm?

So the No Campaign have kicked things off with a two-pronged attack that the guarantees are legally worthless because they are open to interpretation by the European Court of Justice.

Secondly, they argue that the issues dealt with in the guarantees were never the problem in the first place. People have better memories than that. Now arguing that EU law can be challenged by the Court of Justice is from the same dazzling debating school of thought that argues that you can't trust politicians to preserve our power of veto in the future, because they're, you know, politicians. The ECJ can challenge EU law, because it's the highest court in the land and your point? If this is how the campaign is set to proceed, *100 Reasons* isn't holding its breath for a measured adult debate based on the facts. But hey, if it were we wouldn't be able to take the piss out of people anymore, which would make us sad and we'd sulk, so rejoice: the tenor of the debate will be petulant, the information deliberately misleading and the atmosphere increasingly belligerent. Should be fun.

Let's hope that now Biffo has got us the Protocol, he can quietly fade into the background of the Yes Campaign, factoring in the current electoral toxicity of the Fianna Fáil machine... what's the chance of that?!

TL: The Protocols to be attached to the next accession Treaty.

94 Helps the EU to be the bulwark against bad big business practice

The EU will be free to get on with the business of stopping unsavoury business practices as evidenced by the frankly shocking €1 billion fine handed down by the Commission to computer giant Intel.

€1.06 billion?! What did these people do? Feed pesticide to babies? Poke out horses' eyes?

To be exact, it was a €1.06 billion fine levied on the firm for anti-competitive practices, so that makes quite a difference. We'll never round a figure down again. That's a total fine of $1.45 billion dollars or £948 million quid sterling.

The really terrifying thing is that this is like a glancing arrow. If you're pissed off with a company, you fine them a few hundred thousand as a slap on the wrist. If you're appalled by their behaviour, you fine them millions, say about 50. If they're totally unrepentent gangsters, how about €500 million to take the colour out of their cheeks. For instance, in 2004, the Commission fined Microsoft €497 million in 2004 for abusing its dominant market position. But €1.06 billion?! What did these people do? Feed pesticide to babies? Poke out horses' eyes? Run their competitors off the road at lonely mountain passes? Well, let's see...

"Intel has harmed millions of European consumers by deliberately acting to keep competitors out of the market for computer chips for many years," said Competition Commissioner Neelie Kroes. "Such a serious and sustained violation of the EU's antitrust rules cannot be tolerated."

Advanced Micro Devices (AMD) is the rival computer chip company they're accused of deliberately sidelining. The Commission found that between 2002 and 2007, Intel paid off manufacturers and a retailer to favour its chips over AMD's products. It also concluded that Media Saturn, which owns Europe's biggest consumer electronics retailer Media Markt, had been given money so that it would only sell computers containing Intel chips. Intel have denied 'categorically' that it had made pay-offs and vowed to appeal the Commission's findings and 'clear our name and exonerate the company.' Well that puts all the suspicions to rest then, doesn't it? Once a spokesperson denies something 'categorically', well, you can't argue with that.

The Commission found that computer companies Acer, Dell, HP, Lenovo and NEC had all been given hidden rebates to use Intel chips, but not Fujitsu-Siemens, the laptop *100 Reasons* is currently banging out this text on. Ah we feel innocent, exonerated, freshly driven as the melted, wait a second, what's that sticker below the keyboard? A Intel Core™ Duo Inside™ Sticker?! Urrggh, we feel so dirty. We're also appalled by the power of advertising, as when we spotted the sticker, we heard the little three-bar Intel™ bong-bong-bong jingle.

In 2008, Intel made 80.5% of all the microprocessors in PCs, while AMD made 12% with Intel's market share at $85.4 billion with AMD's at $2.6 billion. Both companies are based in California. Intel will pay the fine and be forced to inspect all of its sales deals to make sure that no illegal practices remain. Here comes the clever bit: AMD will not receive any of the fine, which accrues to the EU tax budget. Commissioner Kroes even crowed about this at the press conference joking that Intel would have to change its slogan from 'the sponsors of tomorrow' to 'the sponsor of the European taxpayer'.[115] That chick rocks.

TL: The Lisbon Treaty has no 'Intel Inside', but Intel will be paying for the photocopies.

---

115   BBC website, 13 May 2009

95 The Lisbon Treaty hasn't changed; everything else has.

One thing that the Yes and No sides are in complete agreement about is that the Lisbon Treaty we're voting on in October is the same Treaty we faced last time.

After Cowen had pushed through his wish for the guarantees to become a Protocol, French Premier Nicolas Sarkozy stated to re-assure the rest of Europe: "It is stressed that [the Irish protocol] does not modify in any way the content of the Treaty."[116] This means that none of the other EU countries will have to re-ratify Lisbon.

Despite the guarantees being given cast iron legal status by being upgraded to a Protocol, the 'same Treaty, different year' will be harped on by both sides. The 'different year' aspect is something of an understatement.

Sinn Féin's spokesman on European Affairs Aonghus O' Snodaigh writes "It does not alter the text of the treaty in any way. Nor does it change the impact that the treaty will have on Ireland."[117] At last he understands! Finally. No, afraid not, he tells us the 'clarifications' (yes, I too shudder when I hear that word uttered by a Sinn Féin representative) to the Lisbon Treaty don't address their concerns. Even after the 'clarification' on neutrality, they protest now that their worries about the erosion of neutrality had nothing to do with Irish troop deployment, but were about resources and how it would reflect on us, if other EU countries are involved in military actions. The former political wing of the outlawed, self-appointed, murder-

---

116 *The Sunday Times*, 21 June, 2009
117 *The Irish Times*, 25 June 2009

ous paramilitary 'freedom fighters' we have happily consigned to the tomb of history, is yet again horrified that Ireland might be perceived as a warmonger in the case of France attacking someone. If only they'd always had so much regard for our international reputation.

> If only they'd always had so much regard for our international reputation.

Ah, sure we'd miss their guff, if they campaigned on real issues, wouldn't we? No, we wouldn't. *100 Reasons* has a feeling Sinn Féin are about to find this out come the next election.

TL: no change here.

96 The EU's got funky agencies like the Rapid Alert System for Consumer Goods.

The Rapid Alert System for non-food consumer products (RAPEX) is where EU scientists and technicians get to hang out in their labs testing which irons, power drills and lamps tend to short circuit and set your house on fire and which Chinese toys are likely to kill the dog, if not your entire extended European family.

It's electrical goods, toys and cars that are most likely to be found wanting in minimum safety standards. Although some specific consumer products (like toys, cosmetics, appliances, personal protective equipment, machinery, motor vehicles, etc.) are covered by sector-specific directives, the general requirements apply also to these products when the relevant directives do not provide for a similar rapid information exchange system. We wonder if they're obliged to test *every* product? That could lead to some interesting dinner table conversations for our intrepid EU boffins.

"Honey, what are those burn marks on your arms from?"
"Well, mon ami, I 'ad to test ze new malfunctioneeeng lady shave multi-blade wet/dry depilator". (It's a multinational home).
"And those other, em, suction marks?"
"Ze zucti-o-n marks on my groin are derived from, ow you say, ze 'appiness pump – it is, shall we say, ineffective."

The Head honcho Stefano Soro says "the aim of RAPEX is to make sure that products that pose a health or security risk to consumers do not reach the supermarket shelves. If they've already got there, they will be swiftly withdrawn." [118]

The most common (rapid) measures undertaken are a stop or ban on sales, a withdrawal of a product from the shelves or if necessary, a recall of a dangerous product from consumers. The number of dangerous products withdrawn from the market rose by 16 per cent in 2008 compared to the previous year. Toys top the black list at 38 per cent, while 11 per cent of the list are faulty cars. 59 per cent of the products blacklisted last year came from China, although 20 per cent of the products did come from Europe. Although rather worryingly, 10 per cent of the blacklisted products had 'no known country of origin'. When found, these phantom consumer hazards, made in_____are shipped off to Nepalese orphanages out of sheer badness. [119]

Rather worryingly, 10 per cent of the blacklisted products had 'no known country of origin'.

They group the goods under categories like choking, chemical, electricshock, strangulation and then the catch-all category, 'injuries'. Every Friday, the Commission publishes a report listing the dangerous products reported by the Member States. The lists are terrifying: Christmas lights that are under-insulated, dolls that if licked/sucked have a poisonous chemical risk, hair dyes which contain corrosive skin irritants, high lead levels in toy lipstick ranges... It's enough to make you never leave your house. Wait a second, that's the most dangerous place in the world, so get out if you can still walk.

If you really didn't like someone, were very quick off the mark with your internet shopping and your intended foe was very

---

118   Euronews, 28 April 2009, www.euronews.net
119   You are sick, sick, sick in the head, what sort of people do you think RAPEX are?!

gullible, you could stock their house with precariously mal-functioning consumer goods. *100 Reasons* believes it may just have stumbled across the next big reality TV format: *Acciden-tal Death House* aka *Domestic Jeopardy*. The tagline would be 'most fatal accidents happen in the home: it's more comfy that way.' Just lay back in your defective Laz-ee-boy recliner and watch it on your explosive home entertainment system. Microwave popcorn, anyone?

The system also takes in the European Economic Area coun-tries of Norway, Liechtenstein and Iceland. If you don't want your children to choke on the buttons off their romper suits, it's comforting to know that thousands of products are get-ting spotted and yanked out of the system before anything horrible happens.

TL: It's not a makey-uppey agency, it exists!

97 Joe Higgins will have to engage constructively with EU institutions.

Now that Libertas has imploded and Sinn Féin has lost its seat in Europe, our newly elected Irish Socialist MEP Joe Higgins is the de facto leader of the No to Lisbon II campaign. *100 Reasons* gave Joe its number 3 for Dublin, after Proinsias & Gay Mitchell. He's a subversive influence in European Parliament, but that's why we like him. He's got integrity, he believes in democracy and if Lisbon is ratified, he'll get on with what he's good at – fighting for the unemployed and workers' rights on a bigger stage than he's graced thus far.

Higgins' austere campaign placards of a grainy, black & white, three-quarters length, soberly-suited Joe with shocking pink typescript put the lie to any accusations of champagne socialism here. Our MEP for Dublin offers this self-definition. "I'm a revolutionary socialist. I stand for the complete transformation of society with all institutions, banks and big industry democratically owned and controlled by the people." Joe's going to have fun in Europe.

To see Joe Higgins pip the two incumbent candidates Mary-Lou McDonald of Sinn Féin and Fianna Fáil's Eoin Ryan for the third Dublin seat made it a doubly sweet victory for this underdog. The man whom Bertie Ahern called a failed politician who was espousing a failed agenda has found the correct epoch to launch an attack on the evils of capitalism and on the right-wing cronyism of men like Ahern, who may have been skilful political tacticians, but their failures caused far more casualties and hardship than any of Joe's.

While this socialist shaker may once again find himself breaking down some dance moves in a circle of Turkish workers in
Strasbourg, we doubt that he'll end up serving any hard time in
a Belgian Euro-pokey for blocking Brussels' bin trucks, unless
perhaps they're ferrying away the shredded expense forms of
his less scrupulous Parliamentary colleagues. The man from
the rural farming background in Kerry and the urban teaching
life in Dublin will be able to apply himself to articulating the
needs of farmers and workers both. White collar problems can
be left to someone else. We doubt if ex-seminarian Higgins
cares about any absence of God in the Treaty, as he lost his
faith years ago, probably upon first entering the Dáil.[120]

As is his wont, Higgins has pledged to continue to pay himself only the average industrial wage and donate the rest of his
nearly €90 grand salary to, well, the Socialist party and various
other campaigns associated with the party[121].

Far from a failed politician now, he was the only member of
the No platform to give the perspective any moral or intellec-
tual heft. So here's to Joe, he may be wrong about Lisbon, but
long may he give the robber barons and their political bagmen
sleepless nights. Sometimes, harbouring a few miltant tenden-
cies is just what's needed to get the job done.

*TL: No Joe here, you'll find him instead standing on his seat
at the European Parliament frothing at the mouth at having
no Bertie figure to attack.*

---

120 Profile of Joe Higgins in *Village* Magazine, #36 - 3-9 June 2005
121 We rang them and asked them.

98 It will consign Czech President Vaclav Klaus to the same skip in which the pan-European Libertas party now resides.

The Czech parliament has ratified Lisbon, but President Klaus has refused to sign this decision into law until after the Irish vote. The Czech Republic Council Presidency ran aground half-way through this year when their coalition government under pro-Lisbon Prime Minister Mirek Topolanek collapsed. Much to his glee, this allowed Klaus to assume a much more central role in the last three months of the Czech chairmanship up to July. He appointed a caretaker government under Jan Fischer to see out their European duties until the handover to Sweden.

> It looks like he's read a lot of Orwell and taken him as a prophet rather than a moral commentator on his own time.

Klaus has been shaped by the frustration of the years when his country laboured under communism. After the Velvet Revolution, he was Prime Minister of the Czech Republic from 1992 to 1997 and a Minister for Finance before that drawing on his background as an economics academic, before being elected the republic's second President in 2003, succeeding his main political opponent, the playwright Vaclav Havel. He hasn't had long enough living or ruling a democratic market economy nation to realise the pitfalls of unregulated competition and unchecked nationalism. He views any EU interference in the workings of the market as insulting to the nation state and the first steps to a continent-wide power block delivering dictats to a cowering population. It looks like he's read a lot of Orwell and taken him as a prophet rather than a moral commentator on his own time.

President Klaus is a conservative free-market economist, who refuses to believe that the current depression has anything to do with malfunctions of the market. He has a list of pet hates and bugbears as long as your arm including 'human-rightism', "multiculturalism, feminism, apolitical technoc-ratism (based on the resentment against politics and politi-cians), internationalism (and especially its European variant called Europeanism) and a rapidly growing phenomenon I call NGOism."[122]

Klaus ain't no sissy – he doesn't like environmentalism either. He believes things like global warming are fairytales made up by the liberal media. He said "its main weapon is raising the alarm and predicting the human life endangering climate change based on man-made global warming." He rails against Al Gore's preaching, the IPCC and the Stern report, saying that the measures the environmentalists call to be brought into action will lead to needless de-industrialisation and hamper economic growth. He draws parallels between these campaign-ers and the Soviet economic central planners in their capacity to wreck our chances for prosperity.[123] Yikes. Of course, Klaus never succumbs to alarmism himself: when his predecessor Vaclav Havel invited Salman Rushdie to Prague Castle when he still had a price on his head, Klaus claimed he was jeop-ardising Czech security. We're not saying that Klaus is mad as a box of frogs, just that he's as mad as a gaggle of perfectly rational fatwa-brandishing fundamentalists. Havel referred to his policies as 'gangster capitalism'.

---

122   "View from a Post-Communist Country in a Predominantly Post-Democratic Eu-rope." The Brussels Journal: the voice of Conservatism in Europe.
123   Klaus's website www.klaus.cz The Other Side of Global Warming Alarmism

He gave a speech to the European Parliament in February claiming that the EU was undemocratic. In response, several of the directly-elected MEPs he was addressing walked out. Jo Leinen, the chairman of parliament's constitutional affairs committee, said Klaus presented himself "as a lone and incorrigible provocateur." President Klaus was however sidelined at the June Council Summit, proving unable to scupper the negotiations on the guarantees to Ireland.

Last November, Klaus met with Declan Ganley during his state visit to Ireland and was quoted as calling Foreign Affairs Minister Micheal Martin a 'hypocrite', after Martin called his joint press conference with Libertas after their meeting 'an unfortunate intervention.'

TL: There is no article warning of the variation in quality of Czech Republic Vaclavs.

99 MEPs' expenses have been comprehensively reformed. Or have they?

In the wake of the Commons expenses scandal, it has made sense to Eurosceptics to re-invigorate the row over MEPs' handling of their own expenses. The issue of transparency of allowances available to MEPs has already been addressed by the EP and reforms passed in 2005, but some of its provisions were watered down and doubts remain.

Charges of corruption and 'gravytrainism' (Klaus would like that word) have dogged the European Parliament for decades. A 2009 internal auditor's report was leaked disclosing various scams employed by a number of MEPs. The assistance allowance is worth €17,540 per month or €210,480 per year, which MEPs are allowed to administer through their own firms, without showing how they spent the money. In 2008, Den Dover, the Conservatives' Chief Whip in Europe, was ordered to pay back £500,000 after it was found he had employed his wife and daughter for seven years and paid them £758,146. He was eventually expelled from the party. In June of this year, Giles Chichester, the leader of UK Tory MEPs resigned his chairmanship, when it was found that he'd paid parliamentary assistants' allowances into a family firm of which he is a paid director. He's paid the firm £445,000 since 1996. He didn't feel sufficient pressure to resign as an MEP, though.[124]

A third of British MEPs employed family members. In one case, an MEP paid a staff member a Christmas bonus worth 19 times their monthly salary. Now that's one boss who really

---

124   David Charter, *The Times*, 18 May, 2009

gets into the season's spirit. Some MEPs were paying budget airline fares while claiming for the full price of the flight allowance of up to €1300 for return flights to Strasbourg. The days of merrily booking a Ryanair flight while claiming for first class on Singapore Airlines are over. The travel allowances have been reformed and travel tickets are refunded at face value.

The staff allowances have been comprehensively reformed – allowances now go directly to staff based in Brussels or to an authorised service agency in a members' home state. All payments have to be accounted for and MEPs are no longer allowed to employ family members – although the ones already employed won't have to retire until the end of the next term, which seems to be slow reform indeed.

The salaries of MEPs have been standardised. MEPs used to be paid the equivalent of what parliamentarians in their respective home states earned leading to some massive disparities. This is to stop the practice of expenses being used to make up for these salary differences. All MEPs will get the same rate of €92,000 (well, all apart from Joe Higgins that is.) The Bulgarians must be over the moon. It must have been hard to take, having to listen to some English Eurosceptic bellowing on about how the EU should be taken apart at the seams across the aisle, knowing he was trousering 70 big ones and you were getting a measly 9! No wonder they started skimming. Irish MEPs will be down from what they were on of about 100 grand, but the Lithuanians were on 14 and the Italians, those smooth bastards, were on 140 smackers.[125] The MEPs' controversial second pension will also be phased out.

The Parliament has begun the process of placing on the web the attendance records of MEPs. Ex-MEP Mary-Lou McDon-

---

125   Jamie Smyth, *The Irish Times*, 16 May, 2009

ald wouldn't have liked this much, as even taking her maternity leave into account, she ranked the lowest out of all the Irish MEPs in the last Parliament.

An MEP paid a staff member a Christmas bonus worth 19 times their monthly salary.

Subsistence and general expenditure expenses are still disbursed on a flat rate, so it's clear that further reforms could be pursued. The daily allowance of €292 can still be collected by signing in in the morning, thus collecting it whether you stick around or bugger off for a long weekend of golf, tequila and hula dancers. So after Lisbon has been sent through, the next job is to fully restore public confidence in the expense arrangements for MEPs, even beyond current reforms.[126]

TL: Nope, but we just thought you'd like to know.

126   www.euobserver.com

100 So that Lisbon can get back to being a lovely place and not a byword for tedium

Ever since *100 Reasons* heard the word Maastricht in secondary school, it was shorthand for dull, dull, dull. Right now that dubious association goes to Lisbon. Treaties are never ideal bedtime reading, but Lisbon seems to be taking the biscuit in the all-time-tedious-debate stakes. *100 Reasons* thinks this unfair. We asked Dick Roche about the name. "The word Constitutional Treaty was a very bad mistake. I had a whole variety of views. In fact, one thing was to call it the Dublin Treaty." What?!!!! Our proud capital could've been lumbered with this shit?! He hastened to add "I said, no, no, don't call it that." Phew. "What I wanted to do was call it the People's Treaty." Yes, that would've made all the difference. Anything labelled the People's _____ tends to fall out of favour with the people pretty damn fast, the People's Princess only got the stamp of approval the night she died and even then, it was touch and go. So unfortunately for the people of Lisbon, they had to take the pain.

It's fitting that we end our trawl through the Treaty-to-end-them-all by shuffling off to our Aer Lingus (no Ryanair flights to Lisboa, we're afraid) flight to escape the interminable Irish autumn of the Treaty, safe in the knowledge that our contribution has been rolled up and shoved down the throat of the No Campaign like that porn mag Ian Holm's android tries to choke Ripley with in *Alien*.

Yes, we have no problem portraying ourselves as suffering from delusions of grandeur (our use of the royal we, for instance) and/or as having viscous white pus for blood. It is this albeit faded grandeur that sits well with the Portuguese capital and we leave you, dear reader, ever so slightly envious as we saunter away from you across the sun-dappled cobblestones, before breaking into a jog, scaling a whitewashed stucco wall and parkouring it over the Moorish roofscape of terracotta like Jason Bourne might clamber after a bald-headed assassin. That's how fast *100 Reasons* needs to run from *Lisbon* to arrive in, well, Lisbon.

As you pick your way through the referendum material littering the streets on your way to the nondescript primary school polling station, you can dream of *100 Reasons* chucking a copy of *100 Reasons* from the Bclém Tower, like the detective throwing his badge into the sea (that really happens.)

> You can dream of 100 Reasons chucking a copy of 100 Reasons from the Belém Tower, like the detective throwing his badge into the sea

As you read this, we're sampling the walks over the supposed Seven Hills, we're sipping a coffee at a 'miradouro' lookout point overlooking the bay, we've waving from the yellow tram on our way to the Jeronimos Monastery, where we'llwhile away the afternoon learning titbits about Vasco da Gama. We wonder would the man who opened up the first trade route to India believe in the internal market? And then we'll traverse the long bridge bearing his name that gives San Francisco the pip and head for the pink Pena National Palace that inspired Walt Disney, Brüno and Michael Jackson in wildly contrasting ways. In the evening, the aquarium and the Tile Museum beckon, the latter tracing the development of the tin-glazed ceramic tilework or azulejo... OK, alright, maybe we'll give the fish and the fucking Tile Museum a miss and hit the Bairro Alto district for a wee bit of upmarket R&R after our taxing day and hope that it's better than own puke-stained cultural quarter for a spot of urbane debauchery.

Lisbon's rulers didn't have to manually clear the slums to design a beautiful cityscape like Paris, Nature did it for them. The 1755 earthquake which laid waste to the city, knockeddown the royal palace, 20 churches and two-thirds of the houses. This allowed one part of it, the Baixa, to be planned out on a grid of seven streets. The rest of Lisbon's development has been ramshackle and "as soon as Pombol fell from grace, it resumed its haphazard growth to become the sprawling puzzle it is today."[127] Which is also a pretty good description of the Treaty it lent its name to.

Nevermind, dear reader, if you want to debate the Treaty one more time in the pre-dawn hours of October 2nd, we will make ourselves available to conduct phone interviews from a charming all-night hostelry while listening to a winsome fado singer. The roaming charges aren't prohibitive anymore, so don't hesitate to call and we'll drawl some statistics down the line at you in a spacey, sun-stricken way. So no more 'if you don't know, vote no' – more 'you don't know Lisbon, until you've heard fado.' That's more like it. Fado means *fate* in Portuguese and *long ago* in Irish. To extrapolate - from a long time ago, our fate was to be an integral part of Europe.

100 Reasons thinks that, on mature reflection, we'll drown out this mournful music about unhappy destiny, betrayal and devastating loss by putting on our headphones, select the band, let's see, ah yes, Death Cab for Cutie, and the album? *We have the Facts and We're Voting Yes.*

Press play.

---

127   *Time Out* Lisbon, pg. 28